Co Antrim Vol I
Edited by Donna Samworth

 Young**Writers**

First published in Great Britain in 2004 by:
Young Writers
Remus House
Coltsfoot Drive
Peterborough
PE2 9JX
Telephone: 01733 890066
Website: www.youngwriters.co.uk

All Rights Reserved

© *Copyright Contributors 2004*

SB ISBN 1 84460 512 4

Foreword

Young Writers was established in 1991 and has been passionately devoted to the promotion of reading and writing in children and young adults ever since. The quest continues today. Young Writers remains as committed to engendering the fostering of burgeoning poetic and literary talent as ever.

This year's Young Writers competition has proven as vibrant and dynamic as ever and we are delighted to present a showcase of the best poetry from across the UK. Each poem has been carefully selected from a wealth of *Once Upon A Rhyme* entries before ultimately being published in this, our twelfth primary school poetry series.

Once again, we have been supremely impressed by the overall high quality of the entries we have received. The imagination, energy and creativity which has gone into each young writer's entry made choosing the best poems a challenging and often difficult but ultimately hugely rewarding task - the general high standard of the work submitted amply vindicating this opportunity to bring their poetry to a larger appreciative audience.

We sincerely hope you are pleased with our final selection and that you will enjoy *Once Upon A Rhyme Co Antrim Vol I* for many years to come.

Contents

Ballymacrickett Primary School
Aisling Duffy (11)	1
Clodagh Duffy (11)	1
Anna Brankin (10)	2
Joanna O'Hea (11)	2
Emma O'Neill & Stephanie Campbell (11)	3
Robert Skillen (9)	3
Ben McCambridge (10)	4
Amy McDonnell (10)	4
Michaela Quinn (10)	5
Conor Fitzsimons (9)	5
Siobhán Murphy (9)	6
Conor Hamill (10)	7
Bronagh McGrade (9)	7
Stephen Nelson (9)	8
Lisa McCorry (9)	9
Rosie Mallon (10)	10
Rachel Gourley (10)	10

Balnamore Primary School
Amy Davison (9)	11
Russell Blair (9)	11
Stuart Owler (10)	11
Rachel Davenport (10)	12
Steffan Boyd (10)	12
James McDonald (10)	12
Jonathan Ferris (10)	13
Laura Ellis (9)	13
Charlotte McKendry (9)	13
Curtis McAfee (10)	14
Andrew McAllister (9)	14
Campbell Hunter (9)	14
Shauna Corr (10)	15

Eden Primary School
Chloe Hawkins (9)	15
Lauren Peden (11)	16
Katie Curran (9)	16

Daniel Erwin (10) — 17
Laura Ellison (11) — 17
Emma Kennedy (8) — 18
Corin Keys (11) — 18
Daniel Gordon (11) — 19
Scott Davey (10) — 19
Danielle Lockhart (10) — 20
Katrina Smyth (10) — 20
Michael Reid (9) — 20
Timothy McLean (9) — 21
Frankie Garvey (11) — 21
Gavin Glenn (9) — 21
Megan Patton (11) — 22
Shannen Turner (9) — 22
Amy McInally (9) — 22
Katie Stewart (11) — 23
Matthew Murray (11) — 23
Codie Garvey (8) — 24

Garryduff Primary School
Rachel Love (9) — 24
William Hanna (9) — 25

Groggan Primary School
Rachael Graham (10) — 25
James McKee (10) — 26
Amy Wallace (9) — 26
Victoria Graham (8) — 27
Daniel Gormley (8) — 27
Sheenagh Aiken (11) — 28
Andrew Rainey (7) — 28
Rebecca Herbison (8) — 29
Carla Cameron (8) — 29
Katherine Aiken (8) — 30
Kirsty Wallace (7) — 30
Andrew Hamill (7) — 31
Shannon Wilson (7) — 31
Gareth Millar (7) — 32
Rebecca Nicholl (8) — 32
Hayley Donaldson (11) — 33
Rebecca Nicholl (11) — 33

Alexander Harper (11)	34
Lauren Smyth (10)	34
Adam McIlmoyle (9)	35
Naomi Gregg (11)	35
Naomi Hamill (9)	36
Rebecca Whyte (7)	36
Shannon Cameron (10)	37
Honor Mann (9)	37
Thomas Brown (11)	38
Chloe Buick (8)	38
Xenia Robinson (8)	39
Alana Nicholl (9)	39
Kathryn Cameron (10)	40
Sarah Coulter (10)	40
Mark McMullen (8)	40
Nicole Cameron (7)	41
Nicky Black (8)	41
Aaron McCallister (8)	41
Amelia Kai (10)	42
Victoria Bond (9)	42
Samm Jones (9)	43
Ileanna McDowell (10)	43
Nathan McCartney (10)	44
Kathy Harper (8)	44
Natasha Wylie (10)	45
Sophie McCaw (8)	45
Rachael Kenny (7)	46
Stephanie French (10)	46
Sarah McKee (9)	47

Kilmoyle Primary School

Rachel McKeeman (11)	47
James McLaughlin (10)	48
Adam Millar (10)	48
Alan McKeown (10)	48
James Freeman (10)	49
Alanna Carson (10)	49
Steven Morrison (10)	50
Andrew Brogan (9)	50
Charlotte Millar (10)	51
Hannah Kirkpatrick (9)	51

Jude McCook (11)   52
Sam Kane (10)   53

Landhead Primary School
Nathan Lamont (10)   53
Christie Culbertson (10)   54
Michael Clyde (11)   54
Sarah Hollis (10)   55
Lizanne Wilson (11)   56
Adam McConville (11)   56
Hannah Chestnutt (11)   57
Heather Workman (9)   57
Hannah Campbell (11)   58
Dean Anderson (10)   58
Ben Smith (11)   59
David McClure (10)   60

Mount St Michael's Primary School
Ryan Barry (11)   60
Eimer McGuckian (8)   61
Megan McKenna (7)   61
Ciara Smith (7)   62
Laura Mitchell (8)   62
D'arcy Brady (10)   63
Cathy Mullan (8)   63
Olivia Brown (8)   64
Dervla Robb (7)   64
Nicola Russell (7)   65
Lauren McAreavey (7)   65
Zoe Robb (10)   66
James Martin (8)   66
Shannon Duseath (11)   67
Michael Reynolds (11)   67
Gráinne Dobbin (7)   68
Rachael McClean (11)   68
Kevin Kerr (10)   69
Katie McQuillan (7)   69
Sara Redmond (11)   70
Aine Dolan (10)   70
Jordan McLaughlin (8)   70
Colleen Kelly (11)   71

Amy Steele (9)	71
Emmet Crawford (10)	71
Aoife McGrenaghan (10)	72
Shannon Martin (10)	72
Eilish Dougan (7)	73
Hannah Crilly (10)	73
Medb O'Dolan (8)	74
Bronagh Slevin (8)	74
Conleth McGrenaghan (8)	75
Thomas Devlin (7)	76
James Weir (8)	77
Martin O'Neill (9)	77
Martin Doran (9)	78
Danielle Hughes (9)	78
Seamuis Hanson (11)	79
Joseph Devlin (8)	79
Tony Martin (8)	80
Daniel McAteer (8)	80
Ashleigh Wood (9)	80
Kevin McCann (8)	81
Niamh Magill (8)	81
Sinéad McIvor (9)	81
Richard Fitzgerald (10)	82
Nicole Hazlett (9)	82
Sinead Sweeney (10)	83
Peter Shannon (10)	83
Tara O'Connell (9)	84
Ciaran Carney (9)	85
Owen McGrenaghan (9)	85
Caolan Taggart (9)	86
Aaron Johnstone (9)	86
Megan Dunseath (9)	86
Conor McAuley (10)	87
Danielle Darragh (9)	87
Shéa Conway (9)	87
Michael Dempsey (8)	88
Mairead McCormack (10)	88
Martin Reid (9)	89
Niamh Hanson (10)	89
Kathleen Scullion (9)	90
Séon McCloskey (11)	90
Alanna Cassidy (9)	91

Ryan Boyle (8)	91
Sean Martin (9)	91
Jessica Brown (10)	92
Niamh Molloy (10)	92

Parkgate Primary School

Monty Mackie (9)	93
Sarah Armstrong (8)	94
Scott McCambridge (9)	94
Anna Simpson (9)	95
Patrick Lindsay (10)	95
Caitlin McMillan (8)	96
Gareth Woods (10)	96
Reuben Moore (10)	97
Andrew Higgins (10)	97
Gareth Armstrong (11)	98
Katy Irvine (11)	98
Rebecca McMullan (10)	99
Laura Sloan (10)	99

Rathenraw Integrated Primary School

Thomas Craig (8)	100
Donna-Marie Davidson (9)	100
Shauna Craig (10)	100
Shannon McGreevy (9)	101
Aidan Doyle (9)	101
Paige Havlin (8)	101
Sara Gilmour (8)	102
Calum Reid (9)	102
Rachel Kingsbury (9)	102
Nicola Davis (9)	103
Laura Norman (11)	103
James Gilmour (10)	103
Nathan Gilmour	104
Christopher Robinson (10)	104
Laura Kelly (9)	105
Christopher Heatley (9)	105

St Comgalls Primary School, Antrim

Ciara Dilworth (8)	106
Natasha McMahon (8)	106
Ryan McAuley (9)	107
Martin Gourley (8)	107
Emer McLaughlin (9)	108
Bronagh Lavery (8)	108
Shannen Dilworth (8)	109
Aaron Geoghegan (9)	109
Paul Joyce (9)	110
Aaron Rae (9)	110
Matthew Simpson (9)	110
Matthew Montgomery (10)	111
Ciaran O'Hara (9)	111
Michael Savage (9)	111
Aine McCready (9)	112
Nathan McGarry (8)	112
Alannah McCann (11)	113
Jonathon Smedley (9)	113
Aaron Waring (11)	114
Jack Kelly (11)	114
Conor Butcher (11)	115
Bronagh Shand (11)	115
Desmond Channing (9)	116
Terri-Anne McAlorum (10)	116
Mollie-Claire Somers (10)	117
Siobhan McQuillan (10)	117
Niamh Liddy (10)	118
Niamh O'Connor (10)	118
Maisie Magee (9)	118
Alexandra McDonnell (10)	119
Gemma McErlane (9)	119
Gary Wilkinson (9)	119
Catherine Corrigan (10)	120
Eimear Crilly (10)	120
Jordan Duffy (9)	121
Jack Dalton (9)	121
Ben Johnston (9)	122
Nathan Curtis (10)	122
Ashley Currie (10)	123
Aaron Dalton (9)	123

Naomi Cullen (10)   124
Shannon Connor (10)   124
Sean Caldwell (9)   125
Rebecca Kennedy (9)   125
Dearbháile Liddy (9)   126
Michael Hann (10)   126
Kirstie Crawford (9)   127
India Hunter (10)   127
Lois Brazer (9)   128
Kelsi Waldron (10)   128
Pol McElligott (9)   129
Ciaran Butcher (9)   129
Rachel Taggart (9)   130
Keelan Doherty (9)   130

St Patrick & St Brigid's Primary School, Ballycastle
Ciaran Clarke (11)   131
Darren McGuigan (7)   131
James McLister (11)   132
Bronagh McCaughan (7)   132
Aaron Elliott (7)   133
Christina Torrens (7)   133
Catriona McConnell (7)   134
Riona Lofthouse (7)   134
Ronan Blaney (7)   135
Ciarrai Guihan (7)   135
Stephanie Brown (8)   136
Shauneen Cahill (8)   136
Catriona Donaghy (8)   136
Orlagh McAfee (7)   137
Ruairi Kinney (8)   137
Johnny Black (7)   137
Aine Cunningham (7)   138
Ronan McGuckian (7)   138
Mairead McHenry (7)   139
Daniel McKeague (7)   139
Daniel McPeake (11)   140
Jennifer McHenry (7)   140
Dermot Donnelly (11)   141
Karen McCarry (7)   141
Michaela Murray (11)   142

Shane Devlin (7)	142
Rachael McMichael (11)	143
Karen Hill (8)	143
Caoimhe Hyland (8)	144
Ruairi McKay (8)	144
Alice Mee (8)	144
Megan Mooney (8)	145
Nichola McFaul (8)	145
Abbie McNeill (8)	145
Neill Duncan (8)	146
Megan McHenry (8)	146
Saoirse Hill (8)	146
Brendan Burrows (11)	147
Shannon Hegarty (8)	147
Laura McCaughan (8)	147
Caitilin Gormley (8)	148
Danielle McMichael (8)	148
Rachel McGuigan (10)	149
Alanna O'Donnell (8)	149
Sianine McGowan (11)	150
Hugh Neill (8)	150
Shannen McGarry (11)	151
Diarmaid Hill (10)	151
Maeve McIlroy (11)	152
Jacqueline McAuley (10)	152
Niall Caldwell (10)	153
Gemma Molloy (10)	153
Daniel McKinley (10)	154
Luke Stuart (10)	154
Eamonn McCaughan (10)	155
David Herald (10)	155
Kirsty Mooney (10)	156

Tildarg Primary School

Heather Gault (10)	156
Nicole McConnell (9)	157
Carlyn Tosh (10)	157
Shauna-Lee Warwick (9)	158
Sammi Jo Millar (11)	158
David Kelly (10)	159
Tori Wallace (10)	159

Katie Cummings (9) 160
Emma Patterson (8) 160
Stephanie McDowell (10) 161
Vicki Manson (9) 162
Stuart Patton (9) 162
Susan Bates (10) 163

Tir na Nog Primary School
Jessica Foley (9) 163
Peter Dixon (8) 164
Colette Kelly (9) 164
Samuel McGookin (8) 164
Shannon McCrea (7) 165
Karen Dempsey (8) 165
Fionnuala Carmichael (10) 165
Shannon Neale (8) 166
Erin Fowler (8) 166
Katy Moutray (9) 167
Thomas McGookin (11) 167
Catherine Kelly (11) 168

The Poems

The Mysterious Thing

One day I went for a walk
And I saw this thing,
I thought it looked a bit like chalk,
But then it went *ping!*

I thought it looked like a clock,
But then again maybe no,
Well, it did also go *'pock'!*
And then it gave a sudden glow.

Maybe it was a device,
All the way from the North Pole,
But I suppose it would still be covered in ice
And it would still be cold.

It was nothing I knew of,
Nothing I'd ever seen,
Not anything I'd ever set my eyes on,
It looked like something out of a planet
Where no one has ever been.

Aisling Duffy (11)
Ballymacrickett Primary School

Happiness Is . . .

Happiness is . . .
My favourite meal on my knee,
Spending quality time with my family.

Chatting with my friends on a warm sunny day,
Having a lie-in, in my comfy bed I lay.

Writing this poem has been my pleasure
And now it has become my favourite treasure.

The sound of giggles and laughter too,
The pleasure of helping others and others helping you!

Clodagh Duffy (11)
Ballymacrickett Primary School

My Animals

I love animals, but the bigger I grow
Which one is my favourite? I just don't know
Is it Kim, my jack Russell with her wee fat belly
Or the old noisy donkey my friends call Nelly?
Maybe Thumper, my rabbit - such a cute twitchy nose?
Just lies in the hutch, happy to doze.
Russell, the other wee dog - just mad about the ball,
He has definitely the most energy out of them all.
Jaspers the Lab, is oldest and wisest by far,
He knows who's coming just by their car.
There is Snickers, the guinea pig, all nervous and shy,
Crawls up to your neck and there she will lie,
Like a newborn baby, happy, not a sound,
Just makes me feel the happiest girl around,
I've come to a decision, my mind is at rest,
Not 1, not 2, but all of them *I love best!*

Anna Brankin (10)
Ballymacrickett Primary School

Pets

I've always wanted a cat
Sleek and sly
It would sit behind the table
Until a mouse went by

Or maybe a dog
Barking at the sight of strangers
I would take it to the park
And it would growl at the park rangers

I wish I had those pets
But all I've got is a goldfish
I wish I had them,
I wish, I wish, I wish.

Joanna O'Hea (11)
Ballymacrickett Primary School

Miaow

'Miaow, miaow, miaow,' said the big fat cat.
'Where's my dinner?' purred the big fat cat.
'The dog ate it,' said the rat.
'Why? Why? Why?' said the big fat cat.

He ate his own which was a bone,
He gulped it down just like a stone,
His tummy rumbled and it said,
'I don't want that heavy bone.'
So it began to groan.

He found your food
And was in the mood
To gulp it down just like a clown.
'Oh, I'll get that sneaky dog,' said the cat.

So when the dog got his tea,
The cat ate it and said,
'All for *me!*'

Emma O'Neill & Stephanie Campbell (11)
Ballymacrickett Primary School

God's Love

God's love is red because your heart is red and your blood.
God's love is like the deep blue sea because God's love is deep.
God's love is like the church because that is God's home.
God's love is a beating sound because your heart beats.
God's love is like a circle because there is no beginning or ending.
God's love is like a dolphin because it is deep blue and
                                        God's love is deep.
God's love is like a priest because he minds God's home.
God's love is like the hymn 'The Lord Is My Shepherd'.

Robert Skillen (9)
Ballymacrickett Primary School

My Day After School

At three o'clock I make a dash for the door,
Sliding across the floor,
I run to the bus without a fuss,
Excited about getting home.

When I jump off the bus, I belt up the lane,
Not a care in the world about the rain.
I charge in the house and get my homework done,
Having a nice little cream bun.

After that, anything can happen,
There is the PlayStation, TV, snooker,
Football or even a spin on the quad.

When I'm stopped, I'll have my dinner,
There's a range, which can change,
From bacon to chips, lots, lots more
Lying on the floor.

Then there's boxing which tires me out,
After there's nothing better than to chill out.
The telly does the job
Or playing with my friend, Bob.

I'm soon asleep without a peep.

Ben McCambridge (10)
Ballymacrickett Primary School

My Room

My room is like a jungle
I don't know where to sleep
The clothes are about everywhere
The hamsters underneath

My friend she came for tea once
But she didn't stay for long
'Cause when she came to see me
The mess was ten foot tall.

Amy McDonnell (10)
Ballymacrickett Primary School

My Dog Chelsea

I've always wanted a dog of my own
Because of my asthma Mum said, 'No.'
But after my rabbit passed away,
She changed her mind and said, 'OK.'

We rang her friend who works with a vet
And she said she would find us a pet.
A miniature schnauzer is hard to bet,
Because they are kind, loving and really sweet.

Off to the breeders we set one day,
Excitement was mounting I have to say.
The minute I saw my little bundle of fluff,
I loved her dearly before she barked *woof*.

We had to wait until she was seven weeks old
And keep her snug and warm from the cold.
She loves her new home I'm happy to say,
The day we got Chelsea was a red letter day.

Our lives have changed since she's come,
Although she's a dog we treat her the same.
She's part of the family, we make such a fuss,
Because she has shown so much love to us.

That's why I love *Chelsea*.

Michaela Quinn (10)
Ballymacrickett Primary School

God's Love

God's love is gold like His golden crown.
God's love is like Antarctica's ice because it never breaks.
God's love is like a diamond because it is precious.
God's love is warm like the sun.
God's love is like the sea because it is deep.
God's love is like a cross because Jesus died on a cross.
God's love is like the air because it is everywhere on the Earth.
God's love is like a circle because it never ends.

Conor Fitzsimons (9)
Ballymacrickett Primary School

God's Love

God's love is every colour because when
you are born you see lots of colour.

God's love is like a river because a river
is deep and so is God's love.

God's love is like Heaven because it is
beautiful and so is His love
it is also where He looks down on us

God's love is like crying because when a
baby is born it cries and when someone dies, people cry

God's love is like a circle, there is no
beginning and there is no ending

God's love is like a dog because a dog is
for life not just for Christmas
and that is what love is like

God's love is like Himself because you
don't act like someone, you just be yourself

God's love is like the song
my God loves me because He does love us

God's love is like a red rose.

Siobhán Murphy (9)
Ballymacrickett Primary School

Dan The Frog

There was once a young man
His name was Dan
Whiskey was his favourite drink
But his mother made him pour it down the sink

His best mate was called Sean
And his father's name was John
Dan's second name was Dean
One morning he found a magic bean

He ate it and turned into a frog
When that wife of his saw him
She killed him with a bat!
The next night he was found by the cat
That was the end of Dan the frog.

Conor Hamill (10)
Ballymacrickett Primary School

The Ways We Need Nature

The wind makes a swaying voice blowing all the trees,
The sun makes a quiet whisper, giving food to the leaves,
The people make an eerie echo, repeating for you and me.

The animals wait quietly, camouflaging in long grass,
Whilst the trees blow gently in the wind,
We listen patiently in the town to hear all the sounds.

We need nature, don't you see?
To help us to live and breathe,
We need plants to grow us food
And we need trees to breathe,
We need animals to keep us company
And we need to keep them safe.

Bronagh McGrade (9)
Ballymacrickett Primary School

The Sound Collector
(Based on 'The Sound Collector' by Roger McGough)

A stranger called this morning
Dressed in black and grey
Put every sound into a bag
And carried them away

The cat miaowing for food
The dog barking for a walk
The cows mooing at the dog to go away
The hens clucking for seeds

The baby crying at me
The clock it keeps ticking
The clothes drying up
The toast popping from the toaster

The phone ringing
The doorbell also ringing loud
The light going on and off
The door slamming tight

The chair squeaking
The toaster popping
The plate smashing
The drill putting a hole in the wall

A stranger called this morning
He didn't leave his name
Left us only in silence
Life will never be the same.

Stephen Nelson (9)
Ballymacrickett Primary School

The Sound Collector
(Based on 'The Sound Collector' by Roger McGough)

A stranger called this morning
Dressed all in black and grey
Put every sound into a bag
And carried them away

He took the running of the water
The sizzling of the pan
The swishing of the cloth
And the boiling of the kettle

The crying of the baby
The shouting of the parents
The singing of the girl
And the scream of the boy

The roaring of the TV
The singing of the CD
The loudness of the PS2
The beating of the radio

The purring of the cat
The bubbling of the fish
The barking of the dog
And the nibbling of the hamster

The mooing of the cow
The oinking of the pig
The baaing of the sheep
And the neighing of the horse

A stranger called this morning
He didn't leave his name
Left us only silence
Life will never be the same.

Lisa McCorry (9)
Ballymacrickett Primary School

Happiness Is . . .

Happiness is playing with my cats,
Making sure they don't bring in rats.
Happiness is watching TV,
With the cats on your knee.

Happiness is not going to school,
Sitting at home playing pool.
Happiness is going to the swimming pool,
Going down the slides is so cool.

Happiness is playing in the snow,
Throwing snowballs without hitting Mo.
Happiness is on a sunny day,
Going on the trampoline to play.

Rosie Mallon (10)
Ballymacrickett Primary School

Teachers

T eachers shout, they yell and scream
E ach and every day
A ll they do is chatter
C hatter, chatter and chatter
H ow do we stick it? We don't!
E very day I tell you
R owing on about work like going down a stream
S top the work, stop the talking.

Rachel Gourley (10)
Ballymacrickett Primary School

The Rain Is Coming

Listen, the rain is coming
Banging on the rooftops
Falling on the ground
Making us miserable all around
Yes the rain has stopped
And now we can play
It isn't fair
The rain goes off and on
Now I'll never be able to play again.

Amy Davison (9)
Balnamore Primary School

Rain

Drip-drop, drip,-drop,
Falling on the rooftops,
Splashing on the puddles,
Soaking on the ground,
Going down the drain
And it's dark and dull outside,
Rain, rain, go away,
Come back another day.

Russell Blair (9)
Balnamore Primary School

Winter Haiku Poem

Small snowflakes fall down
Little children play and laugh
And throw big snowballs.

Stuart Owler (10)
Balnamore Primary School

When I Am Upset

When I get upset I feel
Terrible
And destroyed
Miserable
And cross
Upset
And hurt
Annoyed
And stranded in sadness
Then I'm happy again.

Rachel Davenport (10)
Balnamore Primary School

Rainy Day

What a rainy day!
Nothing to do but sit and stare
Oh, what a rainy day!
When the rain hits the rooftops and clitter-clatters
What to do? Nobody knows
If there was something to do
I wouldn't have to sit and stare
Oh, what a rainy day!

Steffan Boyd (10)
Balnamore Primary School

Haiku Poem

Heavy, cold snow falls
Freezing fog comes and cuts the
Snowy cold flowers.

James McDonald (10)
Balnamore Primary School

Rain

Splash, splash, the rain falling,
Pouring down the soggy drains,
Miserable, terrible, dull sky,
It is so cold, we can't go out,
Drip drop, bang,
The rain is soaking.

Jonathan Ferris (10)
Balnamore Primary School

The Rain Will Come And Go

Plip, plop, the rain has stopped
Hooray, hooray, let's go out and play
When we're out
We can dance and shout
But the rain is on again
Boohoo, it was too good to be true.

Laura Ellis (9)
Balnamore Primary School

Wet, Windy, Cold

Drip-drop, splosh splash, goes the rain
Plip-plop, pitter-patter, falling to the ground
Falling down, making puddles wet
Windy, cold, it's a bad day
It's dull, dark and foggy.

Charlotte McKendry (9)
Balnamore Primary School

When I Am Frightened

When I am frightened I start
Shivering
And crying
Quivering
And trembling
Sprinting
And hiding
Shaking
And hugging.

Curtis McAfee (10)
Balnamore Primary School

Rain Is Pouring

Pitter-patter is the rain
Splashing on the ground
And going down the drain
It falls on the fields
And with a clitter clatter
The animals are happy
And they run in the rain.

Andrew McAllister (9)
Balnamore Primary School

What A Miserable Day

Today, today, it's a miserable day
The rain roars like a great lion
What a miserable day!
Drip-drop, splish splash
Pitter-patter, plip plop.

Campbell Hunter (9)
Balnamore Primary School

When I Am Angry

When I am angry I start
Screaming
And kicking,
Yelling
And stamping,
Jumping
And punching,
Exploding
And maddening,
Bashing
And boiling,
Apologising
And hugging,
Sleeping
And making up again.

Shauna Corr (10)
Balnamore Primary School

My Sister

My sister is so lazy
She *really* drives me crazy
All she ever does is eat chocolate bars
And she never ever showers
She thinks she's a little daisy!
I think she's so silly
Because she looks like a Milly
She has a boyfriend called Nick
And he makes me sick
She really likes things that are frilly!

Chloe Hawkins (9)
Eden Primary School

School

School is boring when
You have to
Work, work, work.
School is fun
You get to
Play, play, play.

School is boring when
You have to
Listen, listen, listen.
School is fun when
You have to
Draw, draw, draw.

The worst thing about
School is when
The teacher
Shouts, shouts, shouts,
But the best thing
About school is when
We get to go
Home, sweet home.

Lauren Peden (11)
Eden Primary School

Laddie

My dog Laddie is black and tan
He always does the best he can
My auntie bought him in a van
My sister wanted to call him Dan
My dog Laddie eats lots of meat
And when he is good he gets a treat
Everyone he meets, he always greets
With a big grin to get more treats!

Katie Curran (9)
Eden Primary School

The Squirrel

Here is a squirrel, red and furry,
There he will go, he'll scurry and hurry,
To gather chestnuts
And you should not hear tuts,
'Cause this is all the squirrel has.

Well you might find him up a tree,
Tucking into his nutty tea,
Poor old squirrel withered and slim,
You can nearly see through his bone and limb,
'Cause that is all the squirrel has.

There's no reasons for quarrels
Over squirrels and quarrels and squarrels,
But go out and to the squirrel, feed
Because he will take no great heed,
'Cause it'll help the little squirrel.

So he went into a long, deep sleep,
Until he got back up to jump and leap!

Daniel Erwin (10)
Eden Primary School

What Is It?

I was watching TV in my bed,
When I should have been sleeping instead.

I heard a big bang,
Stuff came down with a clang.

It hid under my clothes,
Then it nibbled my toes

And what do you think I saw?
A big, fat, ugly claw.
Argh!

Laura Ellison (11)
Eden Primary School

A Fantasy Dream House

A fantasy dream house
Painted pink and blue,
A room filled with sweets
And lots of things to do.

A fantasy garden,
A fountain and pool
And even a fan,
To keep me cool.

A fantasy limo,
To take me down town,
I'll go into the mall
And buy a diamond crown.

I know I won't have it,
It's only a dream,
But when I think of it,
I think extreme.

Emma Kennedy (8)
Eden Primary School

I Hate . . .

I hate mornings
It's really up to fate
Whether I stay and lie in bed
And just hibernate

I also hate school
And would like to blow it up
And when it's on the ground in pieces
All the hard school work ceases

I'm not too fond of vampire bats
Their skin's like leather and they never get fat
And when I catch them in the light
I whack them with a different bat!

Corin Keys (11)
Eden Primary School

The Net

First there was the narrowband,
Jogging at slow pace,
It just took forever
To load the results of the race.

Then there was the broadband,
Flying down the line,
It is very fast now,
When it's loading I feel just fine.

Now there is the remote connection,
From anywhere at all,
Even down the park
Or just in the hall.

Soon there will be remote fast lines
And they will be really fast,
But soon they will be slow,
Compared to the next advance.

Daniel Gordon (11)
Eden Primary School

The World

People are blue,
Because of the world turning to goo,
Not with people, not with animals but with crime,
That's why I wrote this rhyme,
This rhyme is not for fun, just don't touch a gun.

This rhyme is just for people to understand
The fear in this year,
To make them aware of crime that is all around,
Be aware or be locked up like a dog in a pound,
That's from me to you to be aware
Of what people would do for a dime.

Scott Davey (10)
Eden Primary School

School Is . . .

School is boring,
School is fun,
School is fun when you muck around
With your chums.

School is boring when you work, work, work,
School is fun when you play, play, play.

Maths is boring, all you do is work,
But using the computer is fun because
You can email your chums.

Danielle Lockhart (10)
Eden Primary School

My Pet Dragon

Oh my pet dragon, he plays with fire,
And he dances about with his own desire.
He leaps and bounds with the greatest of ease,
He flips and dips then does a terrible sneeze.

He hops and flops and smokes like a pipe,
He flies and dives but only at night.
He dances and prances at his own accord,
But best of all this is my pet dragon, the dragon lord.

Katrina Smyth (10)
Eden Primary School

My Mummy

My mummy's a terrible pest
But she always does her best
She stuffs her face with food
She's not often in a grumpy mood
But she's always beautifully dressed.

Michael Reid (9)
Eden Primary School

A Secret

Waiting for the postie to come!
I'm excited, heart booming,
Will I get one?
Watching the door,
Worried it wouldn't appear,
Will there be one for me?
She dipped her hand into her secrets,
A red envelope for Tim,
It's mine!
A valentine.

Timothy McLean (9)
Eden Primary School

The Car

I was walking down the street
And I saw a car
It was red with blue stripes on the side
It also had a giant spoiler
I thought it was cool
I was 18 and I did my driving test
I realised it was parked outside my house
Then I went in
And they said, 'Do you like your new car?'

Frankie Garvey (11)
Eden Primary School

The Carnival

The roundabout is crazy fun
The cake stall sells a sticky bun
The roller coaster is most crazy
But the control man is rather lazy
The carnival is great, it's so much fun!

Gavin Glenn (9)
Eden Primary School

Choices

Dark, smelly, damp
It's like going over a ramp

Black, blue, brown
It's like a very weird crown

Yellow, green, orange
They are very bright

Neon, bright, big
They are my favourites

Lots and lots of fun
That is my favourite one.

Megan Patton (11)
Eden Primary School

The Carrickfergus Castle

Come to Carrickfergus Castle
You'll be *amazed* at what you see
It's time to go exploring
It's the place you want to be
With all its wonderful history
For some it's quite a mystery.

Shannen Turner (9)
Eden Primary School

Report

Mum, before you read that letter
I know I can do better
I am a disgrace
I would pull a face
Remember what I said when you read that letter.

Amy McInally (9)
Eden Primary School

Creepy-Crawlies

Some creepy-crawlies are very vast
Some are slow, some are fast
Some bite hard and sore
Others bite more and more

A few of them smell
And live down a well
Some of them scare me
But not the bumblebee

Nevertheless they're all very nice
But some get eaten by mice
I'm not too keen on ants
It must be very embarrassing when they get in your pants.

Katie Stewart (11)
Eden Primary School

The Monster And His Family

Deep in the mountains in a dark cave,
Lives a monster, his wife and a slave.
The big fat monster only has one eye,
He gave away the other so he could fly.

Now for his wife who has a bad smell,
She can do magic but not very well.
The slave is a vampire who cannot bite,
He cannot fly, talk or fight.

He also has a cat, a big one,
It has a cub, a son.
They're both big and fat
And that's the end of that.

Matthew Murray (11)
Eden Primary School

Bunny

There was once a bunny
That was very funny
He loved lots of money
And ate lots of honey
When he had eaten some stew
That had turned a dark blue
And then came a kangaroo
That hit him with his shoe
Once he met a sheep
That had rather big feet
And went *bleat bleat*
How sweet!

Codie Garvey (8)
Eden Primary School

My Family

My mummy wears thick glasses,
It's because she cannot see,
She took them off the other day
And walked into a tree.

My daddy's really grumpy,
He growled at me last week,
I suppose I cannot blame him,
Since I'd given his nose a tweak.

My sister has got awful warts,
She has them on her toes,
She always says, 'It could be worse,
They could be on my nose.'

Rachel Love (9)
Garryduff Primary School

Mr Turtle

Dear Mr Turtle, how slow you are,
You crossed a river and swam very far,
You met a crocodile and you said, 'Hi,'
Mr Crocodile said, 'You're gonna die,'
'Please don't eat me,' Mr Turtle said,
'Eat that bunny rabbit over there instead.'

William Hanna (9)
Garryduff Primary School

The Baby Who Cried Help!

One day in a little town
There lived a baby in a gown,
Her favourite word was help
Which she would usually yelp.

If there was something she refused to do,
Up the hill she surely flew.
She soon would yelp
'Help! Help! Help! Help!'

Up the hill the crowd did rush
To get the screaming to suddenly hush.
But up there they found
Lying on the ground
The baby rolling round.

Later on that day
Upon the hill, the baby played.
The baby did not see the bog
And tripped over a great big log.

She slid down the bank
And eventually sank,
But the screams of help were ignored.

Rachael Graham (10)
Groggan Primary School

Mystery Frost Man

On frosty nights in the winter,
when it's cold and bitter.
He flies round the houses,
looking for something to ice over with his fingers.
He makes your hands so numb and so cold,
he makes icy paths glitter.
He makes the night nippy,
he makes snowflakes fall from the sky.
He is as sharp as a butcher's knife,
cutting through trees and bushes.
One touch of his fingers,
then ice appears taking over anything in its way.
He makes the leaves crackle.
This mystery frost man is
    Jack Frost.

James McKee (10)
Groggan Primary School

Snow

The snow was like a roundabout
Round and round and round
Fluttering to the ground
I tried to catch the flakes
But they stayed the same every time

You freeze the playground
Just by falling to the ground
You stop the traffic
From going fast

You are great.

Amy Wallace (9)
Groggan Primary School

My Dog

I have a dog called Kate
She's not the cat's best mate

Kate is a collie, black and white
We have to close her in at night

She likes to chase the friendly cats
And even has a look for rats

If they come too near her food
She gets into a really bad mood

She helps with the cattle on the farm
And barks at the birds in the barn

Kate doesn't worry about your good clothes
She likes to sniff them with her dirty nose

Kate is a naughty dog you see
But she's so special just to me.

Victoria Graham (8)
Groggan Primary School

Senses Poem

I like the taste of bacon
Chewing in my mouth

I like the smell of eggs
Sizzling in the pan

I like the feel of ruler's
Hard wood

I like the sound of buses
Starting their engines

I like to see stars
Sparkle in the sky.

Daniel Gormley (8)
Groggan Primary School

Gypsy Gold

Gypsy gold, gypsy folk
Travelling around the globe
One day here, the next day there
With their clothes bright and bold

Gypsy gold, gypsy cart
Trundling along on its way
Ambling gently behind its horse
Chasing after the sun's last ray

Gypsy gold, gypsy boat
Cruising along through the fens
In the country or moored in the town
Gliding along with the wrens

Gypsy gold, gypsy girl
Twirling around in the streets
Feet tapping, hands clapping
The tambourine keeping the beat.

Sheenagh Aiken (11)
Groggan Primary School

Football

Football is my favourite game
Tuesday is the night I train
Saturday is the day of the match
On which my parents come to watch
Giggs is the player I love the best
He plays like a footballer called George Best
Man United is the place to be
So come on down and play with me.

Andrew Rainey (7)
Groggan Primary School

My Little Baby Brother

In the summer we were surprised
Because a little baby brother arrived.
He was small and cute,
Especially wearing his little blue coat.

He doesn't cause much bother,
for his dear old mother.
A drop of milk and a hug,
Then he will play all night on the rug.

Now he is talking,
Soon he will be walking.
What a lovely surprise we got,
I love my baby brother a lot.

Rebecca Herbison (8)
Groggan Primary School

The Seaside

The seaside is a wonderful place,
There's millions of things to do!
Like swimming in the sea,
Building sandcastles,
Going to the shop for ice cream,
Sunbathe on the sand,
Or have a look in the rock pools,
The seaside is a wonderful place,
There's millions of things to do!

Carla Cameron (8)
Groggan Primary School

Mr Alberti

Mr Alberti is the ice cream man
The children would listen for him to come
The music would play
Many a day
He brought joy to many people
I love Mr Alberti!

Mr Alberti is the ice cream man
I love him and his ice cream
He drives about in his van
Selling ice cream
He comes every day
And stops so we can pay
I love Mr Alberti!

Katherine Aiken (8)
Groggan Primary School

List Poem

A good time is going bowling with your family
A good time is having a birthday party
A good time is playing with my toys
A good time is when I go for a walk
A good time is playing with my doll
A good time is doing maths
A good time is having people come to my house
A good time is when I go to the swimming pool.

Kirsty Wallace (7)
Groggan Primary School

Senses Poem

I like the taste of pasta
On my tongue

I like the smell of flowers
In the sun

I like the sound of a bird
In the sky

I like the look of a tractor
In a field.

Andrew Hamill (7)
Groggan Primary School

Senses Poem

I like the taste of bacon
In my mouth

I like the smell of summer
Because it is fresh

I like to feel a cat
Because it is soft and fluffy

I like the sound of the waves
Because they are nice

I like the look of flowers
Because they are blue.

Shannon Wilson (7)
Groggan Primary School

Senses Poem

I like the taste of vanilla
It is my favourite

I like the smell of a sunflower
And it is yellow

I like the feel of a puppy
It is soft

I like the sound from a dog
He barks

I like to see the sky
It's blue.

Gareth Millar (7)
Groggan Primary School

I Can Hear . . .

I can hear people
Talking on the bus
Little children
Making a lot of fuss
Lots of shouting and
Laughing too

Oh dear, oh dear
What is the driver to do?

Rebecca Nicholl (8)
Groggan Primary School

Travelling Through Time

A little boy went back in time
He saw the Romans fighting
And then met an Egyptian girl who was writing
He had so much fun
And even met a Hun

When he got back
He put on his mac
When he found his best mate
He told him he had met an Egyptian girl called Kate
His mate told him, 'Are you mad?
I thought you were a good lad!'
The little boy just carried on
And told his adventure until dawn.

Hayley Donaldson (11)
Groggan Primary School

Don't Mention The V-E-T

The vets are going crazy
Parrots squawking in the corner
Dogs chasing cats
I think I am going because
I can't stand that

I heard cats yelp
And dogs bark like mad
Mice are crawling on the floor
And fish drying out.

Rebecca Nicholl (11)
Groggan Primary School

School

School is fun,
School is great,
I brought a bun
And found a mate.

Outside we play,
We have food,
On a beautiful day,
Nobody is rude.

When it's time to go home,
We watch the telly,
And visit Rome
And fill our belly.

Alexander Harper (11)
Groggan Primary School

The Beach

The waves are lapping on the sand,
The sea is clear and calm,
The breeze is blowing through the trees,
The beach is desolate.

I pick up a shell and put it to my ear,
I can hear the ocean roaring,
The rustling of the leaves on the trees,
The sun is beaming down on me.

Lauren Smyth (10)
Groggan Primary School

Rain

I love the dripping rain,
But sometimes it can be quite a pain!
I like it when it comes and goes
And I get soaked from head to toes.
I like the feel of it
Sliding down my cheek,
I don't like it when
The rain clouds stay
And just won't go away.
That means I
Can't go out and play,
I don't know why,
But I would rather have it,
Than a hot sunny day.

Adam McIlmoyle (9)
Groggan Primary School

Volcano

Red flowing, flowing red
As my mother always said
Scream of pain went through my head
As the hot slow lava ran down
Down, down it came
Towards our town
The lava flowed
Nothing could stop the pain
As the lava came.

Naomi Gregg (11)
Groggan Primary School

Snow Is A Bother

Snow, snow, snow
When will you go?
Why do you stay?
You're here every day
You glisten on the ground
You make me slip around
Snow, snow, snow
When will you go?

When you drop, you melt away
Like a raindrop disappearing
You're always around
Even on my doorstep
You're everywhere!
Snow, snow, snow
When will you go?

Snow, snow, snow
When will you go?
The cars on the road
Are going really slowly
I want to go out
But my mum says no
Snow, snow, snow
When will you go?

Naomi Hamill (9)
Groggan Primary School

My Dog

I have a little dog
His name is Spot
His coat is like a dot-to-dot

He wags his tail
He licks my hand
He is the best little dog in the land.

Rebecca Whyte (7)
Groggan Primary School

A Rainy Day

My favourite sound is to hear the rain pounding against
                              the windowpane,
Pitter patter, pitter patter, the rain hitting against the window
Then it floats down,
Drip drop, drip drop, the rain as it goes down the garage drain,
Splish splash, splish splash, I like to jump in the puddles,
Then as I'm soaked head to toe, I go inside for a warm cup of cocoa
And a change of clothes,
I snuggle down to sleep in front of the fire,
I like to cuddle my dog and hear the lovely sound of . . .
Rain!

Shannon Cameron (10)
Groggan Primary School

A Chilly Morning

Icy roads,
Chilly fingers,
Frosty trees,
Glassy rooftops,
Crisp, crunch, crackling puddles,
Arctic breezes,
Shivering noses,
Rosy cheeks,
Mum shrieks, 'Get up!
Breakfast is ready!'
This is my chilly morning.

Honor Mann (9)
Groggan Primary School

School

This is a hard sum
Why am I so dumb?
It's like my brain is numb
That stupid sum

Art
That's where I'm smart
Not dumb
And I still can't figure out that sum

RE, that's for me
Like Slemish College
That's where there's a bit of knowledge

History
That's an old class
Our teacher's a lass
Who goes to Sunday Mass

Reading
Very leading
That's where I'm a budding seed
Not a dumb weed.

Thomas Brown (11)
Groggan Primary School

Snow

Snow, snow, snow, why do you bother me?
You freeze me like ice, I hate you snow,
When you come you lie there all night and all day,
You can stop the cars,
People can't get to work,
Children are stuck and can't get to school,
Oh snow, I hate you snow.

Chloe Buick (8)
Groggan Primary School

Rain

Drip-drop
The rain is falling off the roof
Onto my window,
Then falling to the ground
Like a bucket of water falling from the sky,
Bursting into little drops,
We like to play,
Splash and flick the rain,
But sometimes we don't like it,
Because it is nippy.

Xenia Robinson (8)
Groggan Primary School

A Drizzly Day

Rain, rain, every day
Day by day rain is there
Look out the window
It looks like a *deluge!*

Very wet, day by day
And then a shower
Just the next day

Now it looks like I'm stuck
With rain, *please*
Not another eight days.

Alana Nicholl (9)
Groggan Primary School

Rain, Rain, Rain

Rain, rain, rain
Oh how I hate the rain
It always comes back again!
Oh how I hate, just hate the rain!
I hate it when there is an absolute downpour
It's so wet it makes me feel sore!
It just pelts down on me
There's nothing I can do about it.

Kathryn Cameron (10)
Groggan Primary School

Rain!

I like to listen to the sound of rain pelting from the sky,
Hitting the rooftops like a deluge,
I think it is pretty,
Watching the rain fall from the sky,
Going drip, drip, drip, I lie in bed at night,
Listening to the sound of rain,
I think it is relaxing,
Listening to it hitting the ground with a thud.

Sarah Coulter (10)
Groggan Primary School

List Poem

Happiness is going home from school
Happiness is not working at school
Happiness is reading books
Happiness is getting a football shirt
Happiness is playing with Andrew
Happiness is playing football.

Mark McMullen (8)
Groggan Primary School

A List Poem

A good time is when me and my friends play all day.
A good time is when we go to school.
A good time is when I go to GB.
A good time is when Sammy and Dad are out of the house.
A good time is when it is Christmas.
A good time is if I get an invitation to a party.
A good time is if I get lots to pick from.
A good time is when me and Kathryn play together.

Nicole Cameron (7)
Groggan Primary School

List Poem

Happiness is playing outside,
Happiness is any bike,
Happiness is football,
Happiness is home-made soup,
Happiness is staying up late,
Happiness is going on holiday,
Happiness is no homework,
Happiness is a cosy bed.

Nicky Black (8)
Groggan Primary School

A List Poem

A good time is a sunny day.
A good time is maths time.
A good time is going on holiday.
A good time is going swimming.
A good time is a new pet.
A good time is going to a zoo.
A good time is going to the beach.
A good time is going to school.

Aaron McCallister (8)
Groggan Primary School

The Rain Is Coming

It's near! It's near!
The rain is coming here
Just look up at the sky
'Now Sarah get your coat
You don't want to get soaked
Get your wellies too
If you get your feet wet
There'll be nothing you can do
Find your hat and scarf
Don't forget your gloves
It'll be really wet if you don't forget.'

Amelia Kai (10)
Groggan Primary School

Rain

I like to hear the raindrops falling on my windowpane
Pitter-patter, pitter
Sometimes the rain's a pain
The way it goes on and on
The only thing is, it is too rainy to be outside
I wish it would stop
Oh I'm beginning to get annoyed
Why, why can't you stop?
It's not just a drizzle, it's a deluge
I'm getting bored staying inside
There's nothing to do, I don't like the rain anymore
It is horrible, why can't you go away?

Victoria Bond (9)
Groggan Primary School

Snow, Snow, I Love You!

Snow, snow, I love you so much,
You're as white as a ghost,
Please, please, keep on falling,
Down, down and down.

Snow, snow, I love you so much,
You are so cold,
But I don't care,
As long as you are snow.

Snow, snow, you are as cuddly as a teddy bear,
Snow, snow, I love you to bits,
But snow, snow, everyone likes you.

Samm Jones (9)
Groggan Primary School

Rain

Rain, rain, I love rain,
Mum, Mum, the rain's begun,
Get my coat, get my scarf,
Out the door I run.
Mum, Mum, the adventure's begun,
Mum, it's time to have some fun,
Swish swash, down the drain,
The rain is getting heavy again.
Rain, rain, I love rain,
Going down my windowpane,
Rain, rain, I love rain.

Ileanna McDowell (10)
Groggan Primary School

The Drum At The Window

I lay awake in my bed
Listening to the rain pelt down on me
It sounded like a great drum
Then there was a cloud burst
I got up and looked out of my window
It was lashing out of the heavens
I got into bed, watching it made me
Feel cold and wet
I pulled the blankets over my head
The tip-tapping was getting louder and louder
Until it started to get annoying
I could not get to sleep, it would just not stop
Then finally it stopped and off I went to sleep.

Nathan McCartney (10)
Groggan Primary School

Snow

It is snowing, hooray, hooray!
Can we play outside?
We can play outside
Only if we put our hats, gloves and scarves on
We are very, very happy and excited
I hope it is snowy tomorrow
If it is, I will build a snowman
It will be very cold
Look, it's snowing
Look at that snowflake swirling and turning.

Kathy Harper (8)
Groggan Primary School

The Best Days Ever Of My Life

I'm a tiny raindrop
And I love to play about
My friends always come to play
I play on the rooftops
Window sills and on the street floor
I make the sounds that people adore
I like to splash, pitter-patter and drip-drop
Some children run in and some run out
Adults run out like lightning to save their washing
But at the end of the day
I end up back home.

Natasha Wylie (10)
Groggan Primary School

The Five Senses

I like the taste of chocolate
Going down my throat.

I like the smell of flowers
Going up my nose.

I like the feel of dogs
As they are soft.

I like the sound of cars
Screaming past me.

I like the look of writing
Because it is so nice.

Sophie McCaw (8)
Groggan Primary School

Senses Poem

I like the taste of sweets
going down my throat.
I like the smell of flowers
in my nose.
I like the feel of my hair
when it is soft.
I like the sound of cars
passing me.
I like the look of a
rainbow in the sky.

Rachael Kenny (7)
Groggan Primary School

A Rainy Day

Rain, rain, rain, it's always such a pain
When I wake up, I always have to make a cup of tea
I hate the rain dripping against the windowpane
Drip drip dripping again
Oh I hate the rain
It dribbles down the drain
Oh how I hate
The rain
The rain
The rain.

Stephanie French (10)
Groggan Primary School

Rain

On a windy, wet night,
Makes me shiver,
When it rains at night,
I hear it pitter-patter on my windowpane,
Splish splash, I hear outside dropping onto the window sill
Then when I woke up the place looked
Like there had been a flood,
I go downstairs to have a better look
And it was up to a metre deep.

Sarah McKee (9)
Groggan Primary School

Blue Days For The Bin Men
(This can be sung to the tune of the Grand Old Duke of York)

Oh our blue bin has arrived
And now we are seeking to strive
To fill it up with our recycling waste
And help our environment survive

Oh we'll try to fill it up
With newspapers, plastic and tins today
And then on Tuesday the bin men will come
And take it to the recycling bay

Oh our class is trying its best
To try and pass the test
Yellow Pages, waste paper and Christmas cards
We've collected without taking a rest

Oh we are on a recycling mission
And it really is our vision
To try and reduce as much of our waste
And make really good decisions.

Rachel McKeeman (11)
Kilmoyle Primary School

Recycle

R educe your waste
E veryone at Kilmoyle can help to have a litter-free school
C ome and join the fun
Y ou can change the way we live!
C ould you help us by recycling your waste?
L ittle amounts of recycling add up to a very large amount
E ncourage everyone to think about recycling.

James McLaughlin (10)
Kilmoyle Primary School

Recycling

Paper, cardboard, plastic and tin
Put them all in your big blue bin
Reducing is the game
Reusing is the name
Recycling is the claim
A better world is our aim.

Adam Millar (10)
Kilmoyle Primary School

Recycling

R ecycle your old stuff, don't throw it away.
E nvelopes and paper can be recycled we say.
C oke cans and other cans can be recycled too,
Y ou can do it, so please, please do.
C an you help us save the environment?
L et's do it now, you know we can.
E nvironment saving is the best plan.

Alan McKeown (10)
Kilmoyle Primary School

Football And Rugby

I like football and rugby

The scoring of lots of goals
And trys

The scoring of lots of brilliant
Free kicks and drop-goals

The great runs to the goal
And try line

The action-packed
And great tricks

The best teams in the world
Playing against each other

I do like football and rugby.

James Freeman (10)
Kilmoyle Primary School

A Wise Boy

Michael was a young boy from Portcin
Whose family got a blue bin
He filled it with paper, cans and plastic
Oh, it really was fantastic
What a smart boy from Portcin

Now my family has started to recycle
Told by a friend called Michael
In goes plastic, cardboard and paper
Also Coke cans and loads of newspaper
So why don't *you* start to recycle?

Alanna Carson (10)
Kilmoyle Primary School

Sounds

I hear the radio singing away
The TV screaming all day
My clock ticking very slow
The PlayStation asks if I'm ready to go

The train puffing at my stop
A car engine starts outside the shop
An aeroplane whooshing in the sky
The ambulance says *nee-naw* in reply

People munching, crunching all their food
A baby crying, now I'm in a bad mood
A plate smashing on the ground
Our cutlery screeching is a horrible sound

What would we do without noise?
We couldn't listen to girls and boys.

Steven Morrison (10)
Kilmoyle Primary School

Mini Beasts

I like centipedes
The glowing red biting type
Munching away at millipedes
Fast and fragile kind
Looking out for predators
I do like centipedes

I like slugs
Sticking like glue to a branch
A slimy path to know the way home
Slimy, sluggish, mushy kind
Munching at leaves
I do like slimy slugs.

Andrew Brogan (9)
Kilmoyle Primary School

Classroom Noise

Listen to the creaking
Cracking of the chairs
Scraping on the floor

Listen to the shouting
And screaming of the children
Playing in the playground

Listen to the creaking
Squeaking of the pens
Writing on the board

Listen to the clunking
Clanking of the footsteps
Stamping on the floor

Listen to the sounds
Some soft, some loud
These are our classroom noises.

Charlotte Millar (10)
Kilmoyle Primary School

Mini Beasts

I like millipedes
The twisting and twirling kind
The wriggles, squiggles kind
The hard back kind with the jelly legs
I do like millipedes

I like ladybirds
The spotty, fluttery kind
The crawling on my hand kind
The black and red type
I do like ladybirds.

Hannah Kirkpatrick (9)
Kilmoyle Primary School

The Luck Of The Dutch

The Holland team were getting ready
All their minds good and steady
Everything was good and on song
Then everything went horribly wrong

Across the road walked Edwin Van Der Sar
Pity he never saw the car
It was a shame about Jaap Stam
He ended up with a 3 match ban

A humble thing happened to Van Nistelrooy
He tripped over his little brother's toy
Luck ran out for Frank De Boer
Broke his leg and that was 4

Reizeger, Davids and Kluivert's luck ran out too
They all ended up catching the flu
You'll never guess what happened to Philip Cocu
He stood on a nail and his face turned blue

Outside went Melchiot and Seedorf
They were chased by a dog back and forth
A crazy thing happened to Marc Overmars
He fell into a really slippery shower

The strangest thing happened to Dick Advocaat
He got attacked by a huge black cat
All of this happened on the week before
The European Championships in 2004.

Jude McCook (11)
Kilmoyle Primary School

My Favourite Mini Beasts

I like pill bugs,
The rolly, fat, fast kind.
They roll into balls,
They climb up walls,
I do like pill bugs.

I like stick insects,
The thin, tall, sticky kind.
They stick to your hand,
They hide in the grass,
I do like stick insects.

Sam Kane (10)
Kilmoyle Primary School

There Was An Old Man

There was an old man who liked big bits of ham,
His name was Pat and he had a fluffy cat.
The old man cooked some ham in his frying pan,
After that he petted his cat.

So the man got into his van,
He was sick of ham so he went to Flash-In-The-Pan,
After that he had to go home and feed his cat,
So Pat went home and fed his cat and that was that.

The next day Pat woke up and fed his cat,
Then he got dressed, he was a bit of a mess.
He got some breakfast and then he remembered
He had to take his tablets,
He sat on the settee and turned on the TV.

Nathan Lamont (10)
Landhead Primary School

Animals

Animals are scruffy
And some are thin and tall,
Some have long tails
And some have none at all.
Some have got sharp teeth,
They use to kill and bite,
Some love to sleep in the day,
Some love to sleep at night,
They hunt and prey in daylight
And no one notices that she is away,
At night she sneaks back in quietly,
To judge if she should eat it,
The prey of the dead mouse.

Christie Culbertson (10)
Landhead Primary School

When The Night Falls

When the night falls, the wind blows
The stars are bright, the stars are shiny
The man on the moon has a nap
And when he wakes up he has a laugh

The moon is big
The moon is wide
The moon is shining
On the sky

When the moon is gone
We are all sad
To see it go
But when it's here
It's a happy day.

Michael Clyde (11)
Landhead Primary School

Animals

A is for ant, small and busy
B is for bear brown and grizzly
C is for camel lumpy and bumpy
D is for dingo wild and grumpy
E is for elephant big and grey
F is for fish that swims away
G is for gorilla who sat on the ground
H is for horse frolicking around
I is for iguana bright and green
J is for jellyfish which makes me scream
K is for kanga and baby roo
L is for lions who live in the zoo
M is for mouse tiny and quick
N is for newt fast and slick
O is for ostrich, its head in the sand
P is for penguin in an icy land
Q is for quail small and neat
R is for robin who looks so sweet
S is for snake with fangs that pierce
T is for tiger who can be very fierce
U is for unicorn a mythical beast
V is for vole who gardeners like least
W is for walrus with her pup
X is for xygore which I made up
Y is for yak a fearsome sight
Z is for zebra all black and white
   These are the animals A-Z
   I think of them all, each night in bed.

Sarah Hollis (10)
Landhead Primary School

The Rainforest

In the rainforest I can see lots and lots of trees,
All the rats running on the ground are infected with fleas.
Every creature has its own sound,
We only know the ones that have been found.
You will see lots of animals that you have never seen before
And scientists believe there are millions more.
Lots of animals depend on their friends,
If one of them dies the circle will end.
You can hear the parrots talking as they fly,
They will meet all the graceful birds flying in the sky,
The rainforest is a wonderful sight,
When you see the animals you will know I am right.

Lizanne Wilson (11)
Landhead Primary School

My Dog

My dog is best,
better than the rest.
He often smells pretty bad,
don't tell him or he will get mad.
He will eat anything in sight,
it would give him a big fright.
His stomach you could never fill,
even if he ate a hill.
His favourite meal is beef,
he takes it from the fridge like a thief.
But the best thing about my doggy,
he really likes to chase a moggy.

Adam McConville (11)
Landhead Primary School

Animals

Any animal big or small
Crazy, vicious
I love them all
Soft and furry
Fat or thin
I love them all from deep within

Some have spots
And some have stripes
And others are black and white
Some they swim and some they walk
Whilst others swing from the treetops

You can hear their roar
It's loud and mighty
And some they sing, delightfully
A rough bark and a soft miaow
A little squeak, quiet and sweet.

Hannah Chestnutt (11)
Landhead Primary School

All About Animals

I love all animals
Big and small
From the tiniest mouse
To a giraffe so tall
There are furry ones
Hairy ones, some with scales
Some with long noses
Some with long tails
The fish live in water
The birds fly
In the sky
Horses roam the hills
And monkeys like to be high!

Heather Workman (9)
Landhead Primary School

The Prince And The Pea

Once upon a time
There was a prince
He thought he could marry
Any girl who had sense
He searched high and low
But found girls who were slow
He wished he was barmy
And threw a big party
His parents went mad
And he thought ah-ha
He slept on a hard pea
And woke up with glee
To find a nurse saying dear me
I thought he was a prince
But his bed makes him wince
She asked him what he would like
He said, 'For all life
I would like you to marry me.'

Hannah Campbell (11)
Landhead Primary School

Birthday Party

I got an invitation to a party yesterday,
It was from my next-door neighbour and it said 'Come and play'.
'I'm looking for some socks, Mum, I can't find a pair.'
Mum shouted, 'Hurry up, Sam,
Oh do brush your hair.'
I'm going to a party,
It doesn't seem fair,
I'll be the only boy
Among all the girls there.

Dean Anderson (10)
Landhead Primary School

Hens And Chickens

Hello, my name is Ben,
I like to chase hens.

They often are fun,
They make you run.

They never are mad
And they never are sad.

They have two legs
And lay for us eggs.

They are hard to catch,
Some eggs can hatch.

This is to stop them from being extinct
And as for their poos, they really stink.

They scratch around
And make lots of sound.

I love hens and chickens,
They're far, far better than Dickens.

I don't really have a favourite,
But I'm impressed with one called David.

Hens and chickens are my fave,
For me they are all well-behaved.

Chickens should be noticed more,
Why can't we just adore.

I absolutely love my chickens and hens,
They love me and they always cluck Ben.

Some folk kill them just for their jobs
And other folk stuff them in their gobs.

Chickens and hens are totally harmless
And somehow they annoy some farmers.

This is where it comes to an end,
Of my little poem about chickens and hens.

Ben Smith (11)
Landhead Primary School

Teacher's Pet

Did you hear a tale of teacher's pet?
Everyone thinks it's me
Miss Henry gets into my car
Every day at three

But did you know it is my cat
She really comes to see
Every day it likes to sit and purr
Upon her knee

I call it Blue but it is grey
It means the world to me
But I would be so very sad
If it got lost or stuck up in a tree.

David McClure (10)
Landhead Primary School

After Dark

I wonder what it's like in the park
When all the lights are off after dark
Probably some insects come out to crawl
While other beasts begin to brawl
There could be a lion in its lair
Enjoying its supper, *a baby hare*
There could be an owl in a tree
Its beady eyes staring at me
There could be a ferocious bear hiding somewhere
But to tell you the truth, I couldn't care
Because there could be an eagle soaring among the stars
Travelling towards *The Beagle* on Mars
This poem it probably needs a better theme
But hey, it's night-time and only a dream.

Ryan Barry (11)
Mount St Michael's Primary School

Touch

Nice warm, silky, satin pyjamas
All year round they keep me warm
Hard, rough, gritty sandpaper
Reminds me of the strong whistling wind
Bumpy polystyrene gives me a very shrivelled feeling
When I scratch it with my nails
Spiky, sharp, wire brush
Reminds me of a prickly hedgehog
A soft spongy sponge
Makes me feel happy and joyful
Hard old lava is very bumpy
Reminds me of the moon
Smooth old pebbles hard and heavy
Makes me think of the beach.

Eimer McGuckian (8)
Mount St Michael's Primary School

Touch

Warm, smooth, satin pyjamas,
Keep me warm and cosy,
Rough, scratchy sandpaper,
Reminds me of thorny bushes,
Polystyrene just like snow except it's not as soft
Sometimes found in walls of houses,
Wire brushes very rough and jaggy,
Feel like prickly thorns,
Sponges oh so spongy and so soft,
Reminds me of my warm relaxing bed,
Lava so hard and so bumpy,
Feels like honeycomb,
Big pebbles feel cold and heavy,
I can't even carry them.

Megan McKenna (7)
Mount St Michael's Primary School

Touch

I love the feel of cosy satin pyjamas
Just as I'm in my comfortable bed

I hate the feel of crispy sandpaper
As it runs through your hands

I love the feel of polystyrene smooth and soft
Just as it runs through my hands
It gives me a lovely thought

I hate the feel of a prickly, sharp wire brush
As it tingles in my hands

I love the feel of a soft bouncy sponge
As it lies there near the sink

I like the feel of stony, crispy lava
As it lands on the table

I love the feel of a smooth hard pebble
I carry it in my hand.

Ciara Smith (7)
Mount St Michael's Primary School

Touch

Warm, smooth, satin pyjamas,
Keep me warm and cosy,
Sandpaper makes me tingle,
When I scratch with my nail,
It makes me shiver,
White polystyrene
Put between the walls to keep us warm,
Also used to keep things from breaking in boxes,
Wire brush used for scrubbing,
Very sharp and bristly teeth.

Laura Mitchell (8)
Mount St Michael's Primary School

The Moon Is . . .

The moon is a 5p coin tossed in outer space.
The moon is a milk bottle lid in a blue bit of cardboard.
The moon is a grapefruit high in the air.
The moon is a banana stuck in the galaxy.
The moon is God's face guiding us and looking down at us
                                                                from the sky.
The moon is a tree with white blossom all over it.
The moon is the FA Cup football kicked high in the air
                                                               by Michael Owen.
The moon will always be a great light source when countries
                                                               are in darkness.

D'arcy Brady (10)
Mount St Michael's Primary School

Touch

Warm, comfy, satin pyjamas,
Keep me snug as a bug,
Rough, hard sandpaper,
Reminds me of the scratching of a nail on a board,
Hard, smooth polystyrene,
In-between walls of a building,
Hard, jaggy wire brush,
Can cut you when you touch it,
Soft, rough sponge,
Washes a car,
Crunchy lava from a volcano,
Smooth pebbles across your skin.

Cathy Mullan (8)
Mount St Michael's Primary School

Touch

Warm, smooth, satin pyjamas,
Keep me warm and cosy,
Rough, hard, gritty sandpaper,
Makes my teeth chatter and shiver,
Warm, soft, dry polystyrene,
Squeaks and squeals
When you rub it with your fingers,
Hard, prickly, tickly wire brush,
Can jag you very hard,
Soft, smooth, spongy sponge,
Stretches and squashes,
Hard, black, gritty lava
Running through my sweaty hands,
Big, hard, rocky pebble,
Heavy, strong and smooth.

Olivia Brown (8)
Mount St Michael's Primary School

Touch

Satin pyjamas keep me cosy,
When I'm in my soft, warm bed,
Sandpaper makes me shiver,
When I scratch it with my nails,
Flat, smooth polystyrene keeps us warm,
In our house between the walls,
Spiky, sharp wire brush
Hurts you when you touch it,
Squeaky, soft sponges
Makes you think of soft pillows,
Pebbles so cold and heavy,
Found on the rocky beach.

Dervla Robb (7)
Mount St Michael's Primary School

Funny Food!

Chilli cabbage
Roaring rice
Ballet biscuits
Choir chips
Quiet croissants
Puppy peas
Boring burgers
Jumbo jelly
Bowling bread
Aiming apples
Chatty cheese
This is silly
Stop it please!

Nicola Russell (7)
Mount St Michael's Primary School

Touch

Warm, smooth, satin pyjamas,
Keeps me cosy in my comfortable bed.
Rough, hard sandpaper,
Reminds me of scratching nails,
Polystyrene smooth, white and lumpy,
Wire brush is like a hedgehog,
Rough and spiky,
Sponge soft and smooth,
Lava rough, hard and lumpy,
Pebble smooth and lumpy,
Reminds me of the rocky beach.

Lauren McAreavey (7)
Mount St Michael's Primary School

My Big Brother, Barry!

My big brother, Barry has a big nose
He always wants to be seen doing a pose

He has curly hair, he used to want to be Lord Mayor
He has hairy legs, he is friends with a man called Begs

When the phone rings it's always for him
He is going out with a girl called Kim
He can't really swim
Because he has a big limb

He usually wears my sister's make-up
And lies in bed all day
He is a good model really
He just has a little waddle!

Zoe Robb (10)
Mount St Michael's Primary School

Touch

Warm, smooth, satin pyjamas,
Keep me warm and snug,
Gritty sandpaper makes me shiver
When I scratch it,
Polystyrene smooth and soft,
Makes me feel like it's snowing,
Wire brush rough and hard,
Makes me think of thorny bushes,
Sponge very soft and smooth,
Lava very hard and light,
Pebbles smooth and cold.

James Martin (8)
Mount St Michael's Primary School

My Sister!

In my room, one of three
I see Megan the little flea
'Get out,' I say
'No, I'm here to stay'
I pack her bags and throw her out
She tries to put on the puppy pout

She's so annoying
She really makes me mad
If Mummy kicks her out
I'll be really glad

I covered her bed in ants
So at night she'd have ants in her pants
It happened that night
She started a fight

She shouts and screams
And calls me names
She never shuts up
And ruins my games.

Shannon Duseath (11)
Mount St Michael's Primary School

Being Me

Being me is very weird
People looked, people sneered
All the boys in school
Reckon they're really cool
But I know that deep inside
I really shouldn't hide
So the next time I see them
I'll stand up for myself
Being cool isn't important, just be yourself.

Michael Reynolds (11)
Mount St Michael's Primary School

Sounds

The sound of the beads rattle,
The slam of a loud door,
The crash of the waves,
The barking of the dogs,
Listen . . . the splash on my window,
The clatter of the dishes.

The crying of a baby,
The ding of a bell,
The flash of the lightning,
The tick of a clock.

The chickens clucking,
Do you hear that? It's a parade!
That is music.

Gráinne Dobbin (7)
Mount St Michael's Primary School

My Friends

Some of my friends are *big*
And some of my friends are small
But I like them *all*

Aisling is the tallest
Seon is the smallest
And the rest are in-between

It matters not if you're big or small
That's *one* difference God gave us all.

Rachael McClean (11)
Mount St Michael's Primary School

Trees In Danger

Trees are beautiful, hard and strong,
Oak trees are steady, big and long,
If trees had legs they would run for their life,
While people cut them down with a knife.

Trees can grow and grow and grow,
In summer their leaves of green always flow,
The apple tree never has any fruit,
For people take them as their loot.

If trees had eyes they wouldn't believe what they'd see,
That's the way it is and the way it has to be,
If trees were alive they would be scared,
As the shout of 'Timber!' can be heard.

Kevin Kerr (10)
Mount St Michael's Primary School

Silly Food

Flying fish
Running rice
Suspicious sausages
Cheerful chips
Cool cabbage
Chatty cheese
Betty biscuits
Pongy peas
String spaghetti
Sweet strawberries
Jumping jelly in my belly.

Katie McQuillan (7)
Mount St Michael's Primary School

What I See Is Important To Me

The sun shines bright,
Everything seems so right,
The trees grow tall,
All the bugs and beetles stay small,
Children make daisy chains,
They hear passing trains,
Down by the sea,
I count the waves,
One, two, three.

Sara Redmond (11)
Mount St Michael's Primary School

The Sea World

The sea is like a bright blue sky
Swirling round the Earth

The fish are like wavy gold ribbons
Lying round the seabed

A sea horse is like a fast taxi
When it's jumping through the seaweed

The sea is full of colourful things
So just come look at the wonderful rings.

Aine Dolan (10)
Mount St Michael's Primary School

The Feel Of Things

I feel the soft leaves
And furry, dry blanket against my skin
The spiky, prickly needles
I like the soft dog
I like the soft seat
My dog is ice-cold.

Jordan McLaughlin (8)
Mount St Michael's Primary School

My Identity

M y name is Colleen
Y ellow is my favourite colour
I live in Randalstown
D ead people scare me
E verywhere things fascinate me
N ice, clever and caring
T o me the world is a wonderful place
I like to eat Chinese
T ogether in my body I make me
Y ou are you and I am me, that is our identity.

Colleen Kelly (11)
Mount St Michael's Primary School

Friends

Friends are like a warm fire on a cold night.
Friends are like a blanket keeping you warm throughout the night.
Friends are like a heart overflowing with love.
Friends are like a puppy staying with you forever.
Friends are like a box of chocolates full of surprise.
Danielle will be my friend forever.

Amy Steele (9)
Mount St Michael's Primary School

The Stars

The stars are God's treasure scattered all over the sky,
They are yellow diamonds in the sky,
They are cat's eyes directing traffic all over the world,
They are God's cameras looking down on us,
They are God's decorations on His Christmas tree,
They are Frisbees flying across the sky,
This is what stars are.

Emmet Crawford (10)
Mount St Michael's Primary School

A Winter's Day

It's a cold winter's day and we're out off to play.
Chimneys are puffing with smoke
And families are huddled around roaring fires.
The footpaths are glistening
And the windows have icicles hanging from them.
Children throwing snowballs like balls of coconuts,
Making snowmen too with great handfuls of snow.
The world is like one big crystal
That will never melt, never go away and never wake.
But one morning waking up to a puddle of water,
No snowman, no ice, just a hat and scarf.

Aoife McGrenaghan (10)
Mount St Michael's Primary School

Boys And Girls

Boys and girls come
Out to play every day
In a sunny day in May
And have fun

Boys think they're cool
So they take days off school
Boys gel their hair and
They stare

Girls do their nails
And never fail
Girls do their hair
Which is fair.

Shannon Martin (10)
Mount St Michael's Primary School

The Feel Of Things

I hate the slimy feeling of seaweed
And the tickly feeling of sand,
I love the feeling of the water as it cleans my feet.

I love the sound of a seashell as it slips out of my hand,
I love the feel of my sister's leather coat
It is soft and cuddly.
I hate the wet house when it is raining,
I love the soft, smooth feeling of chocolate,
I love the furry feeling of sheep's wool,
I love the feeling of the smooth shell as it lets me hear the sea.

I love the feeling of a new teddy as it makes me nice and warm,
I love the feeling of the icicle as it freezes me,
I love the tickly feeling of my bunny slippers,
I hate the feeling of a cold lily pad,
I love the feeling of cold milk as it soothes my throat.

I hate the feeling of pins and needles on my arm,
I hate the feeling of prickly bushes.

Eilish Dougan (7)
Mount St Michael's Primary School

What's . . . Homework?

Homework, homework is a stupid idea
Why, oh why do you exist?

You're just like danger coming to me,
In the night worrying me.

Tonight's the night
I have to do it
Don't worry, don't worry
I'm going to get through it!

Hannah Crilly (10)
Mount St Michael's Primary School

Sounds I Hear

The crashing of the waves
The croaking of a frog
The sound of the radio
The bubbling of a bog
The dull noise of the clarinet
And the clicking of the buttons as you go on the internet

The hoot of an owl
The howl of a dog
The steamy sort of noise that comes from fog
The crunch of the vegetables as you put them up in piles
The rumbling of the engine as you drive for miles and miles

The shouting that's in Burger King as you wait for your food
And the pattering of the rain as you put up your hood

The sound that you hear whenever people talk
And the flapping of the feathers that you hear from the hawk
The splashing of the water in which there is a toad
And the whizzing of a car as it zooms down the road

The crunching of an apple and the miaow of a cat
And the whack of a ball as it hits a baseball bat
The singing of some birds and the quack of a duck
All these sounds could bring good luck.

Medb O'Dolan (8)
Mount St Michael's Primary School

Fear

F rightful images running through my mind
E xits are nowhere to be found
A mixed-up crazy world
R oaring monsters after me.

Bronagh Slevin (8)
Mount St Michael's Primary School

Going Places

When I'm in Tescos I hear lots of things
I hear the beeping of food at the till
I hear the chinking of money purses

I go to Dunnes stores
I hear the humming of the automatic doors
I hear the banging of the clothes hangers
I sometimes can even hear everybody rushing at the January sales

I go to Easons and hear the rustling of the magazines
I hear the crying of a child because he did not get sweets
I hear the banging of the door of the drinks fridge

I go to Super Value and hear the clinking of the trolley change
I hear the shaking of the cereal boxes from a baby who wants them
I hear the chewing from someone with Chewits

I go to Costcutters and hear my mummy talking to the shopkeeper
I hear the humming of the fridge

I go to JJB Sports and hear the rustling of paper inside
                                        some new shoes
I hear the tapping of shoes
I hear the whining sound of my brother wanting new shoes

I go to the joke shop I hear the spring of a bouncy ball
I hear the cackling laughing of the shopkeeper because
                                        of a funny joke
I go to Vivo and hear the splatter of petrol going into the car
I hear the bleeping of the autobank

I go to waves and hear the clattering of dishes
I hear the ring of the bell if people are going past.

Conleth McGrenaghan (8)
Mount St Michael's Primary School

Sounds

On the farm
I hear the dog bark
And the cat's miaows after the mouse
I hear the mouse squeak
And the donkey brays

In the kitchen
I hear the clock ticking
And the clatter of dishes
I hear the chair creaking
And the rubbing of the table getting cleaned

In the bedroom
I hear the books slamming
And the drawers closing
I hear the wind hitting the window
And the bed moving

In the living room
I hear the fire crackling
And the thing smashing
I hear the TV chattering
And the sofas moving

The weather
I hear the wind whistling
And the tapping of the hailstones
I hear the snow crackling

The zoo
I hear the lion roar
And the elephant running
I hear the monkey chitter chatter
People eating
I hear the people slurping ice cream
And the crisps crunching
I hear the crack of battered sausages
And the crunch of Doritos.

Thomas Devlin (7)
Mount St Michael's Primary School

The Feel Of Things

I like the feel of the sharp, jaggy cactus
And the soft furry towel
I like the feel of the prickly back of a hedgehog
And even the feel of the flat soft cloth
I love the feel of a smooth, soft seat

I hate the feel of the rough concrete and hard bumpy beds
I hate the tickly feeling when my sister tickles me
And I even hate itchy feelings
I double hate rock hard ice

I love the feel of sharp lunchboxes
I even like the feeling of the furry mat on my bare feet
I double love soft clothes
I love the glossy smooth sharp pages in magazines.

James Weir (8)
Mount St Michael's Primary School

Sum41

S ee Sum41 singing their heads off,
U p and down the bases go,
M um thinks it's just alright, but I love it.

F orget jazz, it's rock,
O r even heavy metal.
R obbers will want to steal it,
T o my mates I gave it for Christmas,
Y o, you're cool if you get Sum41,
O h you're not going to buy it, well you'll regret it,
N ever play school music but
E normous music like Sum41!

Martin O'Neill (9)
Mount St Michael's Primary School

The Fiddler On The Street

The fiddler on the street,
has tattered shoes and dirty feet.
For every pound, he turns around
and says softly, 'Thank you.'

As he plays his fiddle,
the music flows like a riddle,
sweet and sticky,
like honey from a jar.

As he strokes the strings,
the crowd dance and sway.
Some reluctantly move away,
others remain to listen to him play.

When the police arrive,
he gathers up quickly and hurries away,
Already making plans,
to return another day.

Martin Doran (9)
Mount St Michael's Primary School

What Is . . . The Moon?

The moon is like God eating honey
As it drips off the pots

It is like Mary buttering her toast
And falling into Earth

It is like Mrs Claus eating custard
It's dripping off her chin

It is like Santa Claus sprinkling glitter
On the toys.

Danielle Hughes (9)
Mount St Michael's Primary School

Isabelle

Isabelle, Isabelle sitting in your tree, will you marry me?
Isabelle, Isabelle sitting in your tree, can you see the TV?
Isabelle, Isabelle sitting in your tree, I've got a sore knee
Isabelle, Isabelle sitting in your tree, why won't you mend me?
Isabelle, Isabelle sitting in your tree, got up at half-past three
Isabelle, Isabelle sitting in your tree, watch out for the stinging bee
Isabelle, Isabelle sitting in your tree, upstairs, downstairs
                                        where do you want to be?
Isabelle, Isabelle sitting in your tree, you've got to pay the fee
Isabelle, Isabelle you know it's not free
Isabelle, Isabelle put me in the fire
Isabelle, Isabelle you're a fat liar
Isabelle, Isabelle sitting in your tree, please don't die with me
Isabelle, Isabelle sitting in your tree, why did you leave me?
Isabelle, Isabelle go upstairs
Isabelle, Isabelle say your prayers
Isabelle, Isabelle wrap up tight
Isabelle, Isabelle don't get a fright
Isabelle, Isabelle what a bad night
Isabelle, Isabelle say goodnight
Isabelle, Isabelle turn out the light.

Seamuis Hanson (11)
Mount St Michael's Primary School

Celtic

C eltic is a cool and great team
E xcitement when they score a goal
L arsson is a superb player
T he team always work together
I n Scotland I went to see them
C eltic could win every day.

Joseph Devlin (8)
Mount St Michael's Primary School

WWE Smackdown

W orld Wrestling Entertainment
W atch it Saturday and Sundays
E njoy it

S tone Cold Steve Austin
M assive fights
A ll out after three
C actus Jack
K urt Angle
D own goes Triple H
O n the turn buckle by Jeff Hardy
W on by The Rock
N WO cheats all the time.

Tony Martin (8)
Mount St Michael's Primary School

Soldiers - Cinquain

Soldiers
Fast approaching
Holding their guns tightly
In the darkness of the night sky
Fighting.

Daniel McAteer (8)
Mount St Michael's Primary School

Busted

B and of bad boys,
U for unique,
S for 'School's Out'
T for treacherous
E for envious
D for devils.

Ashleigh Wood (9)
Mount St Michael's Primary School

Sounds

Baby crying,
Someone spying,
Daddy talking in his sleep,
Maria hopping,
Rain dropping,
Lorries tooting, beep, beep, beep.

Mobile ringing,
Teacher singing,
Big sister and boyfriend kissing,
Friends talking,
Feet walking,
My granny's cats are always hissing.

Kevin McCann (8)
Mount St Michael's Primary School

Busted

B ad boys strike again
U se your head and start rocking
S uper cool band
T eamwork rocks!
E is for entertainers
D o get their CD now, it is so class!

Niamh Magill (8)
Mount St Michael's Primary School

Daisy

D ancing ears of velvet,
A lways wanting to play,
I nterested in lots of smells,
S leeps peacefully all night long,
Y aps at the door to get in.

Sinéad McIvor (9)
Mount St Michael's Primary School

The Aliens

The aliens are coming hide under your bed,
Close all the windows and shield your head.

The spaceship looks like a colourful pie,
Up in the dark black sky.

The spaceship lands and the alien comes in,
But in his haste he gets stuck in the bin.

'Give me your sock or I'll blast off your head.'
But when I give it to him he falls down dead.

They're leaving now because they are scared,
Now I think I'm going to scream,
I wake up, oh thank God it was only a dream.

Hey, where's my sock?

Richard Fitzgerald (10)
Mount St Michael's Primary School

The Beast

The beast lives deep in the forest,
Just down the road from me,
He scares me quite a lot,
I hope he's had his tea!

One dark evening,
The beast was sleeping,
Some people sneezed
And then it came seeking.

I heard a piercing scream
And wondered if the beast
Had found the sneezing tourists
And was enjoying a mouth-watering feast.

Nicole Hazlett (9)
Mount St Michael's Primary School

A Perfect Child

A perfect child is nice and kind.
A perfect child loves everyone.
A perfect child is awfully clever.

A perfect child is very pretty.
A perfect child always has pity.

A perfect child is never lazy.
A perfect child never goes crazy.

A perfect child is never late.
A perfect child eats all the veggies on their plate.

A perfect child, hey wait,
Nobody is perfect so that's great!

Sinead Sweeney (10)
Mount St Michael's Primary School

What Are . . . Hailstones?

Hailstones are like a drummer
beating his cymbal.

They are God dropping His snowbell
seeds across the frosty soil.

They are Santa Claus breaking
his glasses with fury.

They are the sound of popcorn
popping in the microwave.

They are the loose stones on a bumpy road
hitting off the back of a car.

Peter Shannon (10)
Mount St Michael's Primary School

Animals

A dog is a pet
It can be
Playful and happy
So it would suit you and me

Cats chase rats
Some are fat
My aunt's cat
Has a special mat

Frogs go *croak*
They also go *hop*
But when they croak
I think they're going to *pop!*

Horses are fast
Some are slow
They do a soft whinny
To say *hello*

Cows are cool
They say *moo*
I know someone
With cows in the zoo!

Sheep are woolly
They say *baa*
The lambs say
Come play, maa.

Tara O'Connell (9)
Mount St Michael's Primary School

What Is The . . . Sun?

The sun is an orange orange
Sitting in a fruit bowl

It is a yellow Smartie
Swimming in my mouth

It is a yellow coloured lemon
Falling from a tree

It is a golden bee
Coming back from a flower

It is an orange disco ball
Swinging in the night

It is an orange cup filling
Up with water.

Ciaran Carney (9)
Mount St Michael's Primary School

What Is The Sun?

The sun is a ruby tomato
falling into a river

It is a yellow clock
floating in the blue sea

It is an orange tunnel
that leads to space

It is a gold star
flying in the sapphire sky

It is a red eyeball
watching you every night in the dark sky.

Owen McGrenaghan (9)
Mount St Michael's Primary School

What Is The Sun?

The sun is a golden melon growing in a fruit garden.
It is a crimson rose floating in the sky.
It is a yellow mess on a blue sheet of paper.
It is a lemon star shining down from Heaven.
It is a honey light bulb lighting up the Earth.
It is an orange placemat on God's table.
It is a group of angels singing in the sky.
It is a yellow leopard dancing in the sky.

Caolan Taggart (9)
Mount St Michael's Primary School

What Is The Sun?

The sun is a golden eye blinking in the sky.
It is a red head setting in the sky.
It is a lemon floating in the sky.
It is an orange kite flying in the sky.
It is a gold lemon hanging in the dark blue sky.
It is a yellow globe floating in space.
It is a red apple setting in the night sky.

Aaron Johnstone (9)
Mount St Michael's Primary School

What Is The Sun?

The sun is a golden ball dancing in the sky.
It is a yellow lemon rolling on a blue table.
It is an orange balloon singing in the rain.
It is a red grape floating in the sky.
It is a fiery blazing flame going up to Heaven.

Megan Dunseath (9)
Mount St Michael's Primary School

The Sun

The sun is a yellow frisbee
Soaring high in the sky

It is an orange lottery ball
Spinning in space

It is the golden yolk in the fried egg
Cooking in the pan

It is a golden plate
Staying high in the sky

It is a blonde football
Kicked high in the sky.

Conor McAuley (10)
Mount St Michael's Primary School

What Is The Sun?

The sun is a fiery star
It is so hot that nobody can touch it
It is a dancing number floating in the sky
It is a round orange squirting heat to the ground
It is a golden face as big as a large round circle.

Danielle Darragh (9)
Mount St Michael's Primary School

Morning Sounds

Birds singing
Water running
Toaster popping
Lorries starting
Morning!

Shéa Conway (9)
Mount St Michael's Primary School

Touching

I like the feel of tickly mats on my feet
The tickly feel of a tree blowing in my face
Or a book rubbing on my back

Do you like the feel of spiky hair?
I do not, it feels like nails on someone's head
I once felt a nettle and it was sore
And it made a white lump on my arm

I love the feel of a blanket around you in bed
It feels like you are sleeping on a sofa
Wool is soft and furry and I like it
The feel of a sheep is nice and I love it

Rough rocks are not good, they are hard
Walls are rough when you touch them and feel them
Rough things are hard and bumpy like stones.

Michael Dempsey (8)
Mount St Michael's Primary School

What Is . . . The Sun?

The sun is a crimson ruby
Shining in the sky.

It is a yellow angelfish
Swimming in the blue sea.

It is a golden disc
Slowly spinning round and round.

It is a lemon ball
Bouncing high in the sky.

It is a fiery button
Floating in the sky.

Mairead McCormack (10)
Mount St Michael's Primary School

What Is . . . The Sun?

The sun is a fiery clock
Floating in the sky.
It is a red globe
Sailing in the sea.
It's a lemon balloon
Flying in the breeze.
It's an orange plate
Spinning in a whirlpool.
It is a gold disc
Swirling in a puddle.
It is a blazing spot
Sailing in the sea.

Martin Reid (9)
Mount St Michael's Primary School

What Is The Sun?

The sun is a lemon ball
Swishing through the blue water.

It is a red apple
Running through the sky.

It is a yellow face
Smiling down at the sea.

It is a ginger honeycomb
Falling into the sand.

It is an orange bobble
Popping out of your hair.

Niamh Hanson (10)
Mount St Michael's Primary School

What Is The Sun?

The sun is a golden beach ball
bouncing across the sky.
It is an orange orange
rolling on the ground.
It is a lemon disc floating
across the air.
It is a big ginger balloon
drifting across the woods.
It is a gold ring spinning
around the world.
It is a yellow bead skipping
across the sea.
It is a blonde face walking
past us.
It is a fluorescent light
brightening up the sky.
It is a yellow fire running
across the world.

Kathleen Scullion (9)
Mount St Michael's Primary School

My Family

My family is a horror,
First your brother's on your phone,
You go to your dad and he says
They're just watching out for you,
Then your sisters take your clothes,
Your mum says you have to share,
What are you meant to do?

Séon McCloskey (11)
Mount St Michael's Primary School

Clouds

The clouds are fluffy white candyfloss
floating in the sky.
God's fluffy chair that He sits on every day.
Marshmallows that the angels have
dropped from the fair in Heaven.
Snowballs caught in the stars,
sometimes they're just clouds.

Alanna Cassidy (9)
Mount St Michael's Primary School

The Stars

The stars are sparks from an angel's bonfire
Angels' eyes watching over us at night
Angel dust which has fallen to light up the sky
Diamonds from angel wands shaken for magic
Coins from the angels' cloaks dropped in the clouds.

Ryan Boyle (8)
Mount St Michael's Primary School

Morning Sounds

Dad's snoring
Toaster's popping
Microwave's buzzing
Mum's groaning
Morning.

Sean Martin (9)
Mount St Michael's Primary School

What Is The Sun?

The sun is a yellow sunflower
that blows in the wind.
It is a golden globe
spinning in space.
It is a flaxen lid,
covering the gateways of Heaven.
It is a lemon football
being kicked from space to Earth.
It is a honey grape
chewed up by the sky and clouds.

Jessica Brown (10)
Mount St Michael's Primary School

What Is The Sun?

The sun is a smiley face,
Beaming rays of happiness upon us.

The sun is a gold dot of paint,
Reflecting down on Earth.

The sun is a fluorescent balloon,
Floating in the air.

The sun is a flashy light,
Brightening the world.

The sun is a yellow tennis ball,
Getting smacked into the air.

Niamh Molloy (10)
Mount St Michael's Primary School

The Last Of The Kings

Once on a battle plain
Beneath the mountain 'Ered Nithu'
There was a clear sight
Of black upon a yellow hue

An army of the dead
From beyond the grave
Had assembled by the river 'Erinave'

The news soon reached the king
Sitting proudly on his throne
And that's how the battle did begin
Of which the minstrels now sing

An army of red and an army of black
Drew swords upon that battle plain
And fought from day to night
But alas, they fought in vain

For a demon forth sprang through
Until, out of the blue . . .

Upon a hill a strong light shone
Of sun glinting upon steel
And then the king charged from the hill
With the noble prince at his heel

He ran up to the demon
And with a mighty thrust
He smote the demon down
Then, he charged the 'king of the dead'

A black arrow was shot through the good king's neck
And his lifeless body flailed
The arrow was the good king's bane
The line of kings had failed.

Monty Mackie (9)
Parkgate Primary School

My Old Dog

My old dog bites postmen new
He even bites my shiny shoe
Rocky is his gallant name
He always likes to play a game

My old dog watches as cars go by
And he ripped up my dad's bow tie
A clever sheepdog was he
But he always got smelly

My old dog always dozes off
Mum cleans up after him with a dirty cloth
He usually chases the cat from next door
He bit me once and it was really sore

My old dog messed up our house
Lots of people say he is as quiet as a mouse
But we knew Rocky we would have to sell
To a farmer who would treat him well.

Sarah Armstrong (8)
Parkgate Primary School

Cats

Cats are clever
Cats are fun
Cats play with everyone

Cats I love
Dogs they hate
But they can't go past the gate

Cats can be quiet
But can make noise
And love to play with their squeaky toys.

Scott McCambridge (9)
Parkgate Primary School

Dogs

Dogs are lovely
Dogs are bright
Dogs are noisy in the night

Dogs are big
Dogs are small
In love with dogs you will fall

Dogs are fat
Dogs are thin
But sometimes they knock down the bin

Dogs can be a real darn nuisance
Even if they're friendly and kind
Caring for them can be a bind

Dogs come in all shapes and sizes
Listen to what I have to say
Love dogs more and more each day.

Anna Simpson (9)
Parkgate Primary School

Dragons

A dragon kills so many men
And gobbles heads off scared hens.
Many soldiers in battle are dying
And leave villages with children crying.

Dragons are fierce,
They carry a dagger's pierce,
Horses have burning hoofs
And houses have flaming roofs,
When the children come out for fun,
They see only ashes as hot as the sun.

Patrick Lindsay (10)
Parkgate Primary School

My Dog Sandy

My dog Sandy is a jolly lad,
I can't think of a time
Where he's ever been bad.

Well, now I can,
It was that funny time
Where he bit the postman.

He's not too slim or too fat,
But he's really scared
Of the next-door cat.

When he first came I was scared,
But I had to pet him
Because I was dared.

He's really cute and fit,
But to tell the truth
I think he has nits.

I find it funny when he twirls,
He's the best dog
In the whole world.

Caitlin McMillan (8)
Parkgate Primary School

My Dog Jade

My dog is a Lakeland terrier
She is called Jade
And she is unafraid

She is seven and a half years old
And at night she gets very cold
She would never get sold

She is my best mate
She'll soon be eight
And she is overweight.

Gareth Woods (10)
Parkgate Primary School

A Scary Ghost

A very scary ghost
Did frighten Mary most
With its tremendous grinning mouth
And large, bold eyes starring out
It floats on air

Mary screams so loud
She turns as white as a cloud
The old ghost roars
Mary's eyes pour

Mum hears all this commotion
She takes out a magic potion
The ghost is scared and runs away
Mary is glad to see a new day.

Reuben Moore (10)
Parkgate Primary School

3rd Street School

School gates open, oh no, here we go,
In through the door and up the hall,
But, by the way, we have a very wonky wall,
All the teachers are real jerks,
That's why we gets lots of homework,
First comes maths, it's a very big pain
And as for our assistant, you would swear he had a mane,
The principal smells like cheese
And keeps a flock of geese,
The lunch bell rings
And *wow!* do these dinners really ming!
Luckily my school is not like that, phew!

Andrew Higgins (10)
Parkgate Primary School

Dragons

Dragons are horrific creatures
With some really ugly features
Their mouth is like a flame-throwing gun
Which is hotter than the sun
They lay giant eggs
As long as one of your dad's legs
The knight so brave
His life he gave
To the sinister dragon

It flew into the sky
Way up high
Their super-hot flame
Will sizzle your hair
Be afraid, be very afraid
Of the sinister dragons.

Gareth Armstrong (11)
Parkgate Primary School

Tyson

Tyson is my boxer
He hunted down a foxer
Even though he's only four years old
He still has a heart of gold
Sometimes he'll come into the house
But one time he brought in a mouse
Now he sleeps out in the shed
And sits there with his gloomy head
I love to take him for a walk
Even though he cannot talk
He runs on ahead of me
Sometimes to where I cannot see
I love Tyson though he can be bad
But if without him I'd be sad!

Katy Irvine (11)
Parkgate Primary School

On Holiday

When I go on holiday
I love being cool
I like to explore the hotel
And jump into the swimming pool

Afterwards I sunbathe
On the golden coast
The kids' club activities
Are what I enjoy most

To buy lots of souvenirs
Is why I go shopping
Spending all my money
I will not be stopping

All of a sudden it's got late
It's time to go to bed
But I think I'll stay up
And have chocolate ice cream instead.

Rebecca McMullan (10)
Parkgate Primary School

Adlough Fern

My dog Fern
Is as black as a blackboard,
He loves the cat
And enjoys a pat.

He works with Dad
And loves to swim,
He is very greedy
And very speedy.

He jumps like a horse
And loves to hunt,
He's gone in a dash
And loves a bath so he can make a splash.

Laura Sloan (10)
Parkgate Primary School

My Toy Box

What's in the toy box?
What's in the box?
What's in the box
With the big brass locks?

There's a Game Boy with games
And some plastic planes,
There are motorbikes
And a man with spikes.

There are plastic towers
And an Action Man with special powers,
There's a falcon that's red
And a furry cheetah with no head.

That's what's in my toy box,
That's what's in my box.

Thomas Craig (8)
Rathenraw Integrated Primary School

Stress

Stress looks like a scary black cat,
Stress smells like dirty feet,
Stress sounds like a rock getting thrown at my window,
Stress feels like a broken heart,
Stress tastes like rotten tomatoes.

Donna-Marie Davidson (9)
Rathenraw Integrated Primary School

Spooky House Haiku

We can stay out late,
We go to our friend's party,
We can have much fun.

Shauna Craig (10)
Rathenraw Integrated Primary School

The Witch's Hallowe'en Shopping Day

Into the shop the witch went and bought
One frog's leg still hopping,
Two bats' wings still cooking in a pan,
Three lizards' legs still walking,
Four spiders' heads with eyes still moving,
Five newts' tails still wiggling,
Six flies' wings still flapping,
Seven dragons' toes still crawling,
Eight crocodiles' jaws still snapping,
Nine dogs' tongues still licking my hand
And ten alligator teeth still chewing.

Shannon McGreevy (9)
Rathenraw Integrated Primary School

Autumn

Leaves falling from the trees,
Squirrels collecting the ripe nuts,
Harvest comes and the pheasant too,
Leaves cracking on the path,
Children collecting the ripe conkers,
People picking apples,
Bright bonfires burning,
Owls hooting in the autumn night.

Aidan Doyle (9)
Rathenraw Integrated Primary School

Happiness

Happiness is like a nice soft cuddly bear,
Happiness tastes like a big fry-up in the morning,
Happiness smells like a bowl of strawberries,
Happiness sounds like birds at dawn,
Happiness feels like a hot bath.

Paige Havlin (8)
Rathenraw Integrated Primary School

A Bird's-Eye View

I am a bird
I fly high in the sky
When I fly over the town
I see people shopping and cars going to a car wash
I hear the water of the car wash

When I fly over the school playground
I smell potatoes, chicken, carrots and peas

When I fly over the beach
I see the children playing
I smell the sea and the seaweed
I hear the waves.

Sara Gilmour (8)
Rathenraw Integrated Primary School

Autumn

The leaves tumble down
Yellow, red and brown
Crunch, crackle and scrunch
I kick them around
My favourite apple pie
My mum made for tea.

Calum Reid (9)
Rathenraw Integrated Primary School

Fireworks Haiku

Fireworks whistle loud,
They go up high in the sky,
Fireworks go bang, bang.

Rachel Kingsbury (9)
Rathenraw Integrated Primary School

I Met . . .

I met a man called Mr McCann
His hair was like elastic bands
And he had really hairy hands

I met a lady called Mrs McBride
Who escaped from the zoo
With a big kangaroo

I met a chid called Little Jack
Who carried his lunch
In a big sack.

Nicola Davis (9)
Rathenraw Integrated Primary School

Autumn

Autumn leaves falling,
Falling from the tree.
Animals hiding,
Hiding in the leaves.
Squirrels are collecting,
Collecting their nuts.
Hedgehogs busy,
Before their winter sleep.

Laura Norman (11)
Rathenraw Integrated Primary School

Hallowe'en Haiku

On Hallowe'en night,
Ghosts and witches come to scare,
On Hallowe'en night.

James Gilmour (10)
Rathenraw Integrated Primary School

The Witch's Shopping List

Into the shop the witch skipped and bought -
One strong bat wing,
Two long frogs' tongues,
Three hairy spider's legs,
Four slimy snakes,
Five sharp eagles' beaks,
Six hard-shelled armadillos,
Seven stinging bees,
Eight colourful butterfly wings,
Nine huge hunchback whales,
Ten furry monkey feet,
Eleven hippopotamus tails,
Twelve sharp bear claws,
Thirteen spotty cheetah skins,
Fourteen stripy tiger teeth,
Fifteen strong lobster claws and
Sixteen leopard spots.

Nathan Gilmour
Rathenraw Integrated Primary School

Autumn

Blow wind blow!
Blow the conkers,
Green spiky ball,
Quickly open it,
Free a shiny brown conker,
Is this the one
To beat the others?

Christopher Robinson (10)
Rathenraw Integrated Primary School

My Toy Box

What's in my toy box?
What's in the box?
What's in the box
With the big brass locks?

There's some super cars
And my sticker stars.
There's a ted called Fred
And a ball that's red.
There's a charming ring
And a picture of a king.
There's a pencil case with rubbers inside
And a doll that once cried.

That's what's in my toy box,
That's what's in the box,
That's what's in the box
With the big brass locks.

Laura Kelly (9)
Rathenraw Integrated Primary School

Autumn

Corn goes in,
Straw comes out,
Out of the thresher
For the farmers,
Farmer Joseph
Works all day,
At night he goes home,
He has apple pie
And crisp sandwiches to eat,
Children are knocking,
Trick or treat.

Christopher Heatley (9)
Rathenraw Integrated Primary School

Windy Nights

The wind whistles
Through the window,
It's running downstairs.
At night
You can feel,
The breeze as
It is rushing by.
At night
It rattles the
Curtains and
Whooshes past,
The TV.
At night
Into the kitchen
Dashing past the
Food and twisting
Out the window and
Out it goes.

Ciara Dilworth (8)
St Comgalls Primary School, Antrim

Summer

Summer, summer
Where are you?
Come, come
Cure my flu.
Stop my sneezes
Achoo, achoo, achoo!
Please, please
Give me a tissue.
Summer, summer
I need you.

Natasha McMahon (8)
St Comgalls Primary School, Antrim

Hands

I use my hands to wave to friends
As they go passing by.

I use my hands to catch the leaves
That fall down from the sky.

I use my hands to tie my shoes
When I go out to play.

I use my hands to wash myself
At the end of every day.

But last of all I use my hands
When I am kneeling down
To pray to God, to watch o'er me
Then not another sound.

Ryan McAuley (9)
St Comgalls Primary School, Antrim

Hands, Hands, Hands

Hands are for building, throwing and catching.
Hands are for giving, holding and scratching.
Hands are for making, writing and praying.
Hands are for painting, plucking and praying.
Hands are for lifting, reaching and shaking.
Hands are for writing, working and baking.
Hands are for feeling, hugging and touching.
Also for gripping, grasping and clutching.
Without your hands there is nothing we can do.
I love my hands, I really do.

Martin Gourley (8)
St Comgalls Primary School, Antrim

Windy Night

Leaves are dashing,
Trees are thrashing
On this windy night.
The floorboard's creaking,
The wind is screaming
On this windy night.
The banshee howling
On this windy night.

Two cats fighting,
Wolves howling
On this windy night.
Grass swaying,
Someone whispering
On this windy night.

Emer McLaughlin (9)
St Comgalls Primary School, Antrim

Daylight

Day is light
But not at night.
Shining sun,
Dull moon,
Bright stars,
Dark clouds.
Stars fill the sky with light,
Clouds fill the sky with darkness,
But the one I like most of all is
When the sun rises.

Bronagh Lavery (8)
St Comgalls Primary School, Antrim

Windy Nights

Lying in bed with lashing winds,
Clashing like a stormy mist,
Roaring like a scary tiger,
Twirling like a thundery tornado,
Crashing like a whispering owl,
Then it rattles through the night,
Thrashing and whooshing as it blows.

Squeaking through the chimneys,
Bashing at the door,
Lashing at the window,
Sighs at the rooftops,
Twisting, swirling and whirling through the clouds.

Shannen Dilworth (8)
St Comgalls Primary School, Antrim

Hands

Hands are used to stroke a pet
To feel a dog's soft fur
And to hold a cat
You use your hands to throw a ball
And hit it with a bat
To pick up leaves in the castle grounds
And to catch the frogs that you've found
You hold a pencil in your hand
And play music in a band
To clap when you see a good show
And wave to people when they go.

Aaron Geoghegan (9)
St Comgalls Primary School, Antrim

Rough And Smooth

Rough is bricks against my fingertips
Rough is rubbing your hand up and down a tree
Rough is sandpaper scraping against the door
Rough is the stony road against my soft shoes.

Smooth is the pebbles in the water fountain
Smooth is the sparkling sand at the beach
Smooth is candyfloss at the fair
Smooth is animals' fur against my skin.

Paul Joyce (9)
St Comgalls Primary School, Antrim

What Does It Remind You Of?

Its wings are like a colourful umbrella
They shine like the sun when they flap about
They feel like soft satin
Its colours are like a piece of art
Its body is soft and silky, tickly as a feather
Just like black velvet
It is a butterfly.

Aaron Rae (9)
St Comgalls Primary School, Antrim

Big Feet

A giant has big feet
About the size of a flock of sheep
I do not know why
It is not the size of a butterfly
But when I said a flock of sheep
I knew a giant had big feet.

Matthew Simpson (9)
St Comgalls Primary School, Antrim

The Sea Behaves In Many Ways

Sometimes it is howling
And the waves come crashing
And bashing onto the rocks.

Sometimes the sea can be
Rough but by the time it
Reaches the beach it is calm.

Sometimes it can be strong
Like a very angry shark
Chasing you onto the beach.

Matthew Montgomery (10)
St Comgalls Primary School, Antrim

What Does It Remind You Of?

Its eyes are like ink on paper
Its body is like hairy jelly beans
Its legs are like obtuse angles
Its legs are as deadly as poison
It is as floppy as a plastic bag in the wind.

It's a *tarantula!*

Ciaran O'Hara (9)
St Comgalls Primary School, Antrim

Windy Nights

I get scared when the wind comes.
I hide in my cupboard.
I watch my window open and close.
The wind is whispering, whistling and roaring.
My mum and dad weren't in the house.
I was in the house on my own.

Michael Savage (9)
St Comgalls Primary School, Antrim

Hands

Hands are great
Hands are fun
We all own our own hands.
They help us work
And they help us play.
They help us wave
To the sun everyday.
They help us wave
Goodbye to friends.
Hands help us say
Our prayers at night.
They help us say
Goodnight to the dark sky.

Aine McCready (9)
St Comgalls Primary School, Antrim

Christmas

Christmas comes once a year
Everyone filled with joy and cheer
Lights burning bright
Lights sparkling in the night
Lots of presents under the tree
Just for you and me
Leave food for Santa
And Rudolph too
I hope he brings me a rally car track
What about you?
Vegetables in the pot
Steaming hot
Snow falling from the sky
Making the ground so white
Let's have a snowball fight.

Nathan McGarry (8)
St Comgalls Primary School, Antrim

Nicola And My Special Friends

N icola is a very good friend
I n the night we play and fight
C an I play with you for the day
O h no we have broken up
L et's get back together and never break up
A fter she slept over we started fighting again.

F riends, friends, mean so much to me
R unning and running to get a drink
I n the night we play at the youth club
E ndless nights we play at the youth club and see each other
N ever see each other until the weekends
D own the road we go shopping
S o we all go back to school and play.

Alannah McCann (11)
St Comgalls Primary School, Antrim

My Day

I go to St Comgalls
It's the best
At the end of each term
We get a test.
I don't like the tests,
They're sometimes hard
I feel like running
Out to the yard.
When it's home time I feel so good
When I get home I ask for food,
When it's bedtime I say my prayers
Then I get sent up the stairs.
I turn off the light
And snuggle up with my teddy bear.

Jonathon Smedley (9)
St Comgalls Primary School, Antrim

Ireland

Ireland is a country
And very small it is
It's produced a lot of talent
Most make it to showbiz

Its nature is so beautiful
It brings tears to your eyes
And if you come and see it
You'll know I'm not telling lies.

And if you're born in Ireland
So very proud you'll be
But I couldn't say the females
Are a pretty sight to see.

But even with all the trouble
Ireland still makes me glad
But of course what do I know?
I'm only just a lad.

Aaron Waring (11)
St Comgalls Primary School, Antrim

The Titanic

T he Titanic took a few years to build
H er first sail was Southampton to New York
E veryone was very excited.

T he Titanic was on its maiden voyage
I ts journey's end at New York
T hat never happened
A great iceberg was looming ahead
N ow it hit
I t broke her in two
C rashed into bits to the bottom of the sea.

Jack Kelly (11)
St Comgalls Primary School, Antrim

Tropical Rainforest

On the forest floor
The jaguars roar
The bugs run
The frogs catch them for fun.

In the understory
The trees are above the quarry
The vines grow high
As the wasps fly by.

In the canopy
The toucan stands proud
The bat's call is loud
The bees flee.

Emergent layer where the birds fly
The mountain gorilla cries
The vines could be snakes
Some birds' beaks could be rakes.

Conor Butcher (11)
St Comgalls Primary School, Antrim

Christmas

Children asleep, tucked up in bed
Waiting for Santa to give the presents
Turkey cooking, waiting for tomorrow
Snow in the sky waiting to fall
Jack Frost waiting to get everyone
Everyone asleep, nature as well
Waiting for Christmas to come tomorrow
Tomorrow will be great
Turkey, chocolate cakes and lovely snacks to eat
Everybody will enjoy the big, snowy day.

Bronagh Shand (11)
St Comgalls Primary School, Antrim

The Sea Behaves In Many Ways

The winds are howling, the sea is screaming.
It is coming up to shore.
The waves are crashing onto the rocks.
The sand is wet.
It is turning brown like a bronze crown.

The sea is silent.
You can hear the air swimming over the waves.

Here we go,
Get your surfboard to have some fun
Up the waves and down again.

The water is cold, the sun is shining.
Walk to the water, it will tickle your toes.

The day has ended, it is raining outside.
We have to stay in.
No more days at the beach for a long, long time.

Desmond Channing (9)
St Comgalls Primary School, Antrim

The Hedgehog

He is like a miniature elephant
Stumbling and tumbling
With his short stumpy legs
He tunnels through the *woods!*

If he's in danger
He turns into a ball of *prickles!*

He is like a fruit-carrier in his ways
But in the light
He is in a pile of dead *leaves!*

Terri-Anne McAlorum (10)
St Comgalls Primary School, Antrim

The Hedgehog

A hedgehog is like the case of a chestnut, only bigger.
With a little pointy snout and a nose like a Malteaser.
He has two tiny eyes like shiny black beads.
He looks so adorable with his little stumpy feet.
Don't be fooled by him though, he's a mean little foe.
He snorts and grunts just like a pig.
At dusk he waddles his way out.
To search for food.
To feed his brood.
He sleeps under a bed of leaves.
To keep warm and safe through the long winter days.
All together you could call him a
Spiky little rustler.

Mollie-Claire Somers (10)
St Comgalls Primary School, Antrim

The Sea Can Behave In Many Ways

The sea can behave in many ways.
It can be calm,
It can be rough,
It can be quiet,
It can be noisy.

When it is rough
It comes crashing and bashing
And roaring in and out
And what is it all about?

When it is calm
It is quiet
Not so bad and not so noisy
I love the sea.

Siobhan McQuillan (10)
St Comgalls Primary School, Antrim

Loneliness

Loneliness is like when you're trapped in a room all by yourself
When you need to talk to somebody but nobody's there.
You can feel lonely anywhere.
When you need somebody but nobody cares.
You feel frightened, alone and scared.
Loneliness is like dark clouds over your head.
There is no sun in your sky.
Loneliness is when there's no one to love you,
Talk to you, share thoughts with you.
Loneliness is like when you're stuck
Between the walls of your room.

Niamh Liddy (10)
St Comgalls Primary School, Antrim

What Does It Remind You Of?

Its wings are as tickly as a feather.
They are coloured like sparkling jewels.
They are all different colours like a rainbow.
Its antennae are like black coals.
Its body is as soft as fur.
Its eyes are like little balls of black wool
It's a butterfly.

Niamh O'Connor (10)
St Comgalls Primary School, Antrim

What Does It Remind You Of?

Its eyes are like small black buttons
Its body is like a bit of black velvet
Its wings are as colourful as a rainbow
And as tickly as a feather
Its mouth is as small as an ant.
It is a butterfly.

Maisie Magee (9)
St Comgalls Primary School, Antrim

What Does It Remind You Of?

Its eyes are light eight little black beads
Its legs are like a gorilla's fingers
Its abdomen is like a black ball of wool
Its feelers are like two steel hooks
It moves like a scurrying crab
It's a . . .
Hairy, scary spider!

Alexandra McDonnell (10)
St Comgalls Primary School, Antrim

Loneliness

Loneliness is when nobody cares about you.
Loneliness is when nobody wants you anymore.
You feel left out in a crowd.
And they don't want to talk to you.
You feel bored when no on will play with you.
You feel like you're lost in a maze and can't find your way out.
That's what loneliness is.

Gemma McErlane (9)
St Comgalls Primary School, Antrim

What Does It Remind You Of?

Its eyes are like snooker balls
Its skin is as an evergreen tree
Its legs are like a ruler
It can jump about two feet in the air
The croak reminds me of nails scratching on a chalkboard
It moves as quick as a snake
It's a *frog.*

Gary Wilkinson (9)
St Comgalls Primary School, Antrim

The Seaside

At the seaside there was seaweed
It was spread everywhere
A dog on a lead
And a granny in a wooden chair.

There were seagulls flying in the sky
The jellyfish sting when you walk by
There is a gentle breeze in the sky
Children playing in the sun
They're also having fun.

People are collecting shells
In the sunny spells
The adults are getting a tan
And the children are at the ice cream van!

Catherine Corrigan (10)
St Comgalls Primary School, Antrim

The Small Stout Brussels Sprout

I'm a stout little sprout
sitting on a shelf.
I'm feeling very frightened
because I know what might happen.

Peeled, chopped, boiled or steamed,
I don't know what they'll do.
I hope I'm not the first one picked
to sit on a plate near you.

Bye-bye friends, no doubt I'll see you soon
sitting right beside me on a silver spoon.

Eimear Crilly (10)
St Comgalls Primary School

The Hedgehog

The spiky thief lumbers in your garden
He sometimes kills the slugs and snails
And sometimes makes a terrible mess.

So look out for a ballish, spiky thing
And it might be a hedgehog.

I call him the prickly pig
He is a hoover for the slugs and snails
He can also roll up in a ball
And push out his spines when danger comes near.

He always plays stupid
By crossing the road
So let him get flattened
He's only a hedgehog.

Jordan Duffy (9)
St Comgalls Primary School, Antrim

Gangster Dude

The prickly, round cushion comes in the garden
The thief steals all the food
He scuffles through the bin
He rolls in tight balls to defend himself
He cleans and hoovers the garden with his mouth
He is the gardener's friend.

He is not intelligent when it comes to roads
He can eat poisonous snakes and bees and wasps
He has a leathery nose and a pointy snout
He hibernates in winter until March comes.

Jack Dalton (9)
St Comgalls Primary School, Antrim

In The Dark

In the dark I feel scared
Because I can see
The shadows of trees.

I can hear noises
From next door
And creaks from my sister running about
I can also hear the pipes creaking
Which is scary.

I sometimes feel relaxed
And then I hear something
Falling and then I jump up
And look around.

It is also scary when
Someone knocks on the door
I think it is someone
Trying to *frighten* me.

Ben Johnston (9)
St Comgalls Primary School, Antrim

Holidays

H appy children in the summer
O utside playing water fights
L ay in bed every day
I ce-cold ice cream to cool us down
D iving into the water every day
A t my cousin's house playing on his skateboard
Y ellow ducks in the water
S izzling sun in the sky.

Nathan Curtis (10)
St Comgalls Primary School, Antrim

The Round Chubby Red Thing!

I am an apple
A juicy red apple
Living on a green tree with all my friends.
I used to be a blossom
Now just ripe and awesome
I never want to be picked . . .
Apples say a young apple got eaten by
Harry Snedwick.
He is very scary.
He's the fattest boy on Earth
As he comes each day to search
For apples on our tree.
I sure hope he doesn't pick me!
Here he comes now . . .
Arghh!
Stop that! It hurts!
Munch, munch, munch
Crunch, crunch, crunch.

Ashley Currie (10)
St Comgalls Primary School, Antrim

Holidays

H ot and sunny every day
O utside in the sun playing games with your friends
L ight nights every night
I ce lollies to keep you cool from the sun
D iving in the swimming pool that is cool
A way!
Y ellow bright sunshine in your eyes
S it in the shade to get away from the sun.

Aaron Dalton (9)
St Comgalls Primary School, Antrim

The Seaside

The sand is hot
And the sun is shining
Fishermen are fishing
And children are sitting
In the sand, playing.

The seaside is fun
The bright sun is shining
In the sky
I wish I was at the seaside.

The sun is going down
The children are going home
The fish are going under
The jellyfish are going under the water.

Naomi Cullen (10)
St Comgalls Primary School, Antrim

I Am A Carrot!

I am an orange carrot,
I grow down in the soil,
The farmer looks after me,
With lots of care and toil,
My body grows down under,
My head grows up above
And when I am bright and orange
The farmer pulls me out,
He sends me to the shop,
For everyone to see,
Then people come and buy me
And then cook me for their tea.

Shannon Connor (10)
St Comgalls Primary School, Antrim

Windy Night

Whistling in the chimneys,
Bashing at the doors,
Circling the roads,
The wind roars and roars.
Howling in the distance,
Swishing through the night,
Crashing at the windows,
Swirling in the sea,
The wind wakes me.

Squealing over the hills,
Breaking through the seas,
Howls at my door,
Twisting through the seas.
Rattles at my window,
Clashing at the walls,
The wind wakes me.

Sean Caldwell (9)
St Comgalls Primary School, Antrim

Holidays

H aving fun in the sun.
O utside in the cool pool.
L ying at the poolside getting a tan.
I n a nice cool tub.
D ining out on the balcony.
A lways being red and brown.
Y ellow sand on the beach.
S unbathing all day long!

Rebecca Kennedy (9)
St Comgalls Primary School, Antrim

P6 Thoughts

I was feeling so excited
We were going back to school
Just to see my friend again
Oh I hope our teacher's cool.

I'll be loaded down with books again
There'll be lots of tests I know
The work will be so hard this year
The 11+ must go.

I know I'm not the brightest brain
And I'm going to find it tough
So I'm going home to Mummy 'cause
Right now I've had enough.

Dearbháile Liddy (9)
St Comgalls Primary School, Antrim

Scared Without Light

Scared in the dark without a light
Trembling in fear
Thinking there's somebody there.

Clutching your blankets
With shivering hands
The cold wave travelling
Up your spine.

Hearing voices like growling wolves
Or a man with a bloody knife.

Rustling leaves and branches
Chills out of control crouching
And curling up into a ball
That how I feel in the *dark!*

Michael Hann (10)
St Comgalls Primary School, Antrim

The Crunchy Gonner

I am an apple
A crunchy, green apple
Waiting on a supermarket stall.

I am in a bag with all my friends
I hate this awful bag
But still I will be bought soon
Thank goodness.

My friends *frighten* me
With terrifying stories
They say I will be eaten in a pie.

Oh no! I've just been bought
Now they are going to eat me
I'm a *gonner*
Arghh!

Kirstie Crawford (9)
St Comgalls Primary School, Antrim

Loneliness

Loneliness is grumpy faces.
No one there to tie your laces.
Loneliness is not looking pretty.
Living in this big, tall city.
I'm scared.

Loneliness is having no friends.
Loneliness is having no one to feed you.
You don't get presents.
Loneliness is bad.
Sometimes you can even go mad!

India Hunter (10)
St Comgalls Primary School, Antrim

Windy Nights

Sometimes when it's windy
And it's the scariest of nights
Our tree's hit the power lines
And out go all the lights
My sister's only little
And she gets quite a fright
The house all lit with candles
It really is quite a sight
We all jump into one bed
And have a pillow fight
And I tell spooky stories
Well into the night
Then finally we sleep
We hold each other tight
Until the morning comes
And everything's alright.

Lois Brazer (9)
St Comgalls Primary School, Antrim

Loneliness

Loneliness is feeling lost
Loneliness is being neglected
No one to help you
No one to check your homework
You walk around with a frown
And everyone else is smiling
You're all alone, nobody to care
You feel unloved, you feel unsafe
And you think to yourself
Could my life have been better
And why am I so angry?

Kelsi Waldron (10)
St Comgalls Primary School, Antrim

Windy Nights

Thrashing the chimneys
Dashing down the stairs
Screeching like a cat
Swishing through my room
As fast as a witches broom
Rattling at my door
The wind howls like a dog
This is the wind at night.

Lashing through the sea
Squealing like a baboon
Thrashing at my window
Flashing down the stairs
Whispering to my dad
This is the wind at night.

Pol McElligott (9)
St Comgalls Primary School, Antrim

Windy Nights

Rustling down the chimneys
Rattling up the stairs
Squeaking in my bedroom
Whispering in my ear
Roars in the hall
Dashing in the kitchen
Going out my door.

Running in the streets
Lashing like a dog
Blowing my toys away
Thrashing the deep blue seas
Twirling round and round
Falling on the ground.

Ciaran Butcher (9)
St Comgalls Primary School, Antrim

Windy Nights

Whooshing in the chimneys
Rattling down the hall
Smashing glass in the kitchen
Rushing through the window
Rustling through the trees
Rumbling on the rooftops
Flying through the door
Yes, it's the wind
It is squeaking round
My bedroom door.

The wind blows through the trees
The wind mutters in the sky
Lashing against the window
Running through the sky
Crashing through the clouds
Howls from the owls
Nothing can stop it
It's the crashing
Wind.

Rachel Taggart (9)
St Comgalls Primary School, Antrim

Blue

Blue is a big, blue whale
Blue is the sky
Blue is like a big abyss
Blue is a deep sea
Blue is smart like my mum and dad
Blue is neat like me.

Keelan Doherty (9)
St Comgalls Primary School, Antrim

The Noises Of The Night

I was lying in my bed
Pretending to be dead
In case of a fright
In the middle of the night
I open my eyes
And get a surprise

People on the street
Stamping their feet
Phones ringing
Like people in the pub singing
People talking on the landing
Where the creepy plant was standing.

The noises of the night
All give me a fright
But these noises are in my head
For I am safe in my bed.

Ciaran Clarke (11)
St Patrick & St Brigid's Primary School, Ballycastle

My Hands

I love my hands because . . .
They can stroke a furry, friendly cat
Dip in a pond and catch a fast fish
And eat from a dish
They're good to hold a big iron bar
They can stick up a poster of your favourite star
They can make a mould of a man out of clay
But the best part of all
Is when they grip a rope to help me play.

Darren McGuigan (7)
St Patrick & St Brigid's Primary School, Ballycastle

Noises In The Night

Lying in my bed
Eyes shut tight
Had a good day but not a great night
All around I hear noises
this is the house at night.

Lying in my bed
Noises in my head
Floors creaking
Doors squeaking
This is the house at night.

Lying in my bed
All around me there are
Pipes banging,
Toasters popping
Phones ringing,
Taps dripping
This is the house at night.

James McLister (11)
St Patrick & St Brigid's Primary School, Ballycastle

My Hands

I love my hands, they can . . .
Push and pull a speedy sleigh
Make a beautiful Bronagh being made from clay
Pin a physical picture onto the wall
Play a terrible tune on the tuba or the trombone
Save a great goal
Break your favourite toy and mend it again
Now it's time to start all over again!

Bronagh McCaughan (7)
St Patrick & St Brigid's Primary School, Ballycastle

My Eyes

I like my eyes
They can look
They can read a brilliant book
They can cry when I am sad
Get smaller when I am mad
See the time on the clock
Admire colours of the peacock
Stare at the perfectly tuned piano
Squint my eyes at the bright yellow sun
My eyes can blink and give a wink
One goes when I wink
Two go when I blink
I love my eyes.

Aaron Elliott (7)
St Patrick & St Brigid's Primary School, Ballycastle

My Mouth

I love my mouth because . . .
It talks to my mummy
It can kiss my cats
It can yell at my brother
It can eat sweets off a placemat
It can drink water and juice
It can spit on the ground
It can laugh at my friends
I can move up and down
I can kiss my dad
It can taste things like crisps or buns
It can chew on some sandwiches and pull faces that are fun.

Christina Torrens (7)
St Patrick & St Brigid's Primary School, Ballycastle

My Hands

My hands can move all over the place
I can touch my nose that's on my face
They can grip a ball
And if I trip they break a fall
They can carry a sweet to my lips
When I dance I touch my hips
They can write
They can write words in a poem
And cuddle my favourite garden gnome
They can draw a pretty rainbow
And join clothes together when I sew
I love my hands.

Catriona McConnell (7)
St Patrick & St Brigid's Primary School, Ballycastle

My Hands

I love my hands because they can . . .
Make and bake a lovely cake
Hold the book when I cook
Grab a big fish on a shiny dish
Use a bat and give it a whack
Hit a ball at the wall
Pull a rope for a tug of war
They smack and clap together when I rap
And I shake and bend the hands of my friends
I just love my hands because . . .
They can do lots of things.

Riona Lofthouse (7)
St Patrick & St Brigid's Primary School, Ballycastle

My Hands

I love my hands they can . . .
Stroke a furry cat
Put on my hairy hat
Grip a bouncy ball
Help me when I fall
Clap very loudly at something good
Hold a knife and fork when I eat my food
Hit very hard
Wiggle my fingers in a wave
Great goals they save
Touch nice and horrible stuff
Tell me if things are smooth or rough.

Ronan Blaney (7)
St Patrick & St Brigid's Primary School, Ballycastle

My Hands

I love my hands because . . .
They can push a shopping cart along the mall
Cup my mouth when I call
Smack together in a clap
Roll out my favourite giant map
Play with the computer in my house
Type on the keyboard and click the mouse
Write a poem on some paper
And then draw a picture later.

I love my hands.

Ciarrai Guihan (7)
St Patrick & St Brigid's Primary School, Ballycastle

My Hands

I love my hands
They pick a bunch of red roses
They stick on eyes and stick on noses
They build sandcastles out of sand
Rock a baby in a pram
They sweep up leaves and take home shopping
Hold my dog's lead when we go walking.

Stephanie Brown (8)
St Patrick & St Brigid's Primary School, Ballycastle

My Mouth

I love my mouth because it can . . .
Eat lots and lots of lovely things
Cheer up my friends when I sing
Taste food that are sour or sweet
Like ice cream that is my favourite treat
Tell jokes that are funny
And give a big kiss to my mummy.

I love my mouth.

Shauneen Cahill (8)
St Patrick & St Brigid's Primary School, Ballycastle

My Mouth

I love my mouth because it talks to my mummy
Eat sweets that go to my tummy
Can kiss my dad
Can yell when I am bad
Can sing songs quietly or loud
Into a smile when I am proud
I love my mouth.

Catriona Donaghy (8)
St Patrick & St Brigid's Primary School, Ballycastle

My Mouth

I love my mouth because . . .
It talks to Mummy.
Proclaims, I've got an empty tummy.
Let me explain.
When I am mad,
Shows I'm happy and glad,
Laughs at funny stories and songs,
Shouts when I speak to my dad,
Whispers into my friend's ear when she is sad.
I love my mouth.

Orlagh McAfee (7)
St Patrick & St Brigid's Primary School, Ballycastle

Midnight Hunter

The barn owl flies out into the night
And gives all the mice a fright.
His wings spread and his feathers are white.
He swoops over mice with a silent flight.
You can't see him in the trees.
When he sees a mouse it should flee.
Pygmy shrews and mice beware, beware.
He could be anywhere.

Ruairi Kinney (8)
St Patrick & St Brigid's Primary School, Ballycastle

Yellow Feels Lucky

Yellow looks and smells like a lion,
King of the beasts.
It's like an enormous jar of honey.
Yellow feels like a pot of gold.
Yellow sounds like the luckiest thing in the world.

Johnny Black (7)
St Patrick & St Brigid's Primary School, Ballycastle

My Hands

I love my hands because . . .
They do lots of things
Like save the best goal
Wave goodbye
Carry a piece of gold
Wipe my tears when I cry
They cover my work
Write a magnificent poem
And pin it to the wall
They can break a toy
Clap along to a show
Cram buns into my mouth
Tie my ribbon into a bow.

Aine Cunningham (7)
St Patrick & St Brigid's Primary School, Ballycastle

My Hands

I love my hands because they . . .
Can tie knots in shoelaces,
Open the door to new places,
Fold paper into a plane,
Grab my friends in great games,
Flutter fingers when I wave,
Stop great goals when I save,
Pull a trolley and push a ball,
Pin a page upon a wall,
They can do a lot of things,
Like my favourite game, catching.

Ronan McGuckian (7)
St Patrick & St Brigid's Primary School, Ballycastle

My Hands

I like my hands they can do lots of things
They can . . .
Stroke a cosy cat
Hit with a big bat
Shake some marvellous maracas
Make some monstrous monsters out of clay
Fold a piece of paper
Hold my big brown bear tight
Grab a bouncy ball
Pin a picture on the wall
Push a baby down the hall
Save a great goal
Put grip on a stick
Help Mum when she is sick
Wave bye to my friends
Pull my red coat on to go for a walk
Share sweets I give out at Hallowe'en
Cover my eyes then I say . . . 'Boo!'
Steer a steering wheel
Break an ornament it's no big deal
And burst bubbles that's great
Now you see why I love my hands
They're my mates.

Mairead McHenry (7)
St Patrick & St Brigid's Primary School, Ballycastle

The Colour Yellow

Yellow looks like the hot sandy desert.
It sounds like a dress swaying.
Yellow feels like a smooth wood.
It tastes like a banana.
Yellow smells like chips.

Daniel McKeague (7)
St Patrick & St Brigid's Primary School, Ballycastle

Fright

I'm lying in my bed, I hear the phone ring
I answer it, no response.
Then the doorbell rings, no one is there.
I see a light on my mirror
Is it the microwave?
No, it's just the moon
This is the house at night.

I hear scratching on the floorboards.
I hear a door creaking and a branch hits my window.
A draft goes down my back and I shiver.
This is the house at night.

My heart goes *thump, thump, thump*
And my eyelids go *boom, boom, boom* very gently.
I close my eyes and curl up with the blankets around me.
Yes, this is the house at night.

Daniel McPeake (11)
St Patrick & St Brigid's Primary School, Ballycastle

My Hands

I love my hands because they can . . .
Save a great goal
Pet a baby foal
And they can bring in coal.
They can steer a baby down the hall
Break a fall so I don't get hurt at all
And they can throw a ball.
They can pin a page on the wall
They can help me stretch up really tall
And they can help me call.

Jennifer McHenry (7)
St Patrick & St Brigid's Primary School, Ballycastle

Sounds At Night

Is that the rustling of leaves
Or is that a gang of thieves.
Is that the rain
Or someone knocking on the windowpane?

Is that my dad snoring
Or is that the thunder roaring?
Is that the door creaking
Or is that my mum screeching?
Yes, this is the house at night.

Is that the lashing of rain
Or is that my sisters crying in pain?
All I can do is hope I can fall
Into a very deep sleep,
Yes, this is the house at night.

Dermot Donnelly (11)
St Patrick & St Brigid's Primary School, Ballycastle

My Hands

I love my hands, they can . . .
Pin a page on the wall.
Help to bounce a ball.
Carry ice cream to my lips.
Wave goodbye.
Dry tears from my eyes.
Break a fall so I won't be hurt at all.
Write a story that's full of life and glory.
Pick apples from trees.
Makes me a card from me to you.

Karen McCarry (7)
St Patrick & St Brigid's Primary School, Ballycastle

Night-Time

I don't really like the night,
There's something about it
Which gives me a fright.

The toaster popping.
Things dropping
Drip-drop
Tip-tap
Something sends shivers down my back.

Creak, creak,
Eek, eek
A monster is coming,
I hear humming.
My images take me by surprise
I suddenly see these great big eyes.
I have to fight and be ready,
Oh, it's just my teddy!

Michaela Murray (11)
St Patrick & St Brigid's Primary School, Ballycastle

My Hands

I love my hands
They can hold a bouncy ball
Use a bat to strike it hard against the wall.
Write a list poem about my hands.
Hit a drum when I play in my band.
For my tea, they hold my cup and biscuit
Put them to my mouth so I can take a bit.
Plays the PlayStation game 'Ratchet and Clank'.
Kills the baddies
And gets the hydroysphaser back in a blink.

Shane Devlin (7)
St Patrick & St Brigid's Primary School, Ballycastle

The House At Night

Lying in bed with clothes pulled tight.
With eyes wide open
No sleep in sight
I hear a noise in the dark
Coming from the park
Or perhaps it's a dog bark?
This is the house at night.

A creak from the floorboards
Sends a shiver down my spine
Suddenly there's a tapping at the windows
As the moonlight glows
This is the house at night.

Is there someone in my room?
I see shadows on the wall, large and scary
Oh *phew,* it's only the mirror
This is the house at night.

Rachael McMichael (11)
St Patrick & St Brigid's Primary School, Ballycastle

Barn Owl

The barn owl's out at night.
You can see him swoop in his silent flight.
Barn owls show white underneath their wings,
You never know what the barn owl brings
He looks for mice and other things.

Creatures of the night *beware!*
Owls can give you such a scare.
The owl could catch you with his claws.
Gobble you with hungry jaws,
Scurry away with your fast little paws!

Karen Hill (8)
St Patrick & St Brigid's Primary School, Ballycastle

The Best Barn Owl

The barn owl flies out in the night.
He sleeps in a barn when it's daylight.
He likes to hunt when the moon is bright.

He spreads his wide wings out very long.
He eats lots of food so now he's strong.
We love to see him glide.
He flies across the field with pride.
When he flies home he likes to have a rest.
He's the best barn owl, yes, he's the best.

Caoimhe Hyland (8)
St Patrick & St Brigid's Primary School, Ballycastle

Harvest Acrostic

H ibernating animals.
A pples are ripe.
R ed leaves.
V egetables are ready.
E veryone works.
S carecrows in fields.
T ractors and trailers.

Ruairi McKay (8)
St Patrick & St Brigid's Primary School, Ballycastle

The Silent Hunter

The barn owl hunts in the dark night.
He likes to hunt when the stars are bright.
Tonight there is a bright moon.
He'll be back with something soon.
He spreads his wide and silent wings.
His chicks wonder what food he'll bring.

Alice Mee (8)
St Patrick & St Brigid's Primary School, Ballycastle

Night Hunter

The barn owl doesn't fly in light,
It flies at night.

Swoops through the skies,
Just like a ghost he flies.

His heart face looks so grim,
If you're doing something you'll stop to see him.

He wonders what the night will bring,
When morning comes he goes home on silent wings.

Megan Mooney (8)
St Patrick & St Brigid's Primary School, Ballycastle

Happiness Is Yellow

Yellow looks like a field full of sunflowers.
It sounds like a canary bird singing.
Yellow feels like a budgie.
It tastes like bananas and lemons.
Yellow smells like a lovely daffodil.
The fields are full of yellow buttercups.
In the morning there is a golden sun shining upon the fields.

Nichola McFaul (8)
St Patrick & St Brigid's Primary School, Ballycastle

Yellow Things

Yellow looks like the summer sun shining in the sky.
It sounds like a warm sea breeze.
Yellow feels like fluffy baby chicks.
It tastes like honeycomb.
Yellow smells like buttercups.

Abbie McNeill (8)
St Patrick & St Brigid's Primary School, Ballycastle

Yellow Narnia

Yellow sounds like the lion in Narnia.
Aslan roars and sorrow is no more.
It tastes like the magic apple.
It cured the sick mother.
Yellow smells like toffees in the sun.
That grew into a toffee tree.
Yellow looks like magic.
Yellow feels like a sleigh.
The witch rides away.

Neill Duncan (8)
St Patrick & St Brigid's Primary School, Ballycastle

White Wings The Owl

He sleeps in a barn when the sun is bright.
In the night he comes with the soft moonlight.
He wonders what prey the night will bring.
Mice and a lot of other things.
He spreads his white and silent wings.

Megan McHenry (8)
St Patrick & St Brigid's Primary School, Ballycastle

Yellow

Yellow looks like butterflies and sunflowers.
It sounds like baby chicks cheeping.
Yellow tastes like honey.
It feels like fur on a line.
Yellow smells like lemon juice.

Saoirse Hill (8)
St Patrick & St Brigid's Primary School, Ballycastle

My Life Without A PlayStation

My life without a PlayStation
Would be a wreck night and day
I would have nothing to do
And nothing to play.
My favourite game is GTA 3
You go flying about in a car
'Cause you're free as can be.
Another one is MTV Music Generator
You make songs
It's the game to tell you where hip hop belongs.
Last but not least is James Bond Agent Under Fire
My brother thinks I cheat and calls me a liar.

Brendan Burrows (11)
St Patrick & St Brigid's Primary School, Ballycastle

Yellow Is Beautiful

Yellow looks like daffodils.
It sounds like dry sand.
Yellow feels like fluffy chicks.
It tastes like an egg yolk.
Yellow smells like sunflowers.

Shannon Hegarty (8)
St Patrick & St Brigid's Primary School, Ballycastle

I Like Yellow

Yellow looks like a glowing star.
Sounds like a baby chick crying.
Feels like a cold bowl of vanilla ice cream.
Tastes like a banana milkshake.
Smells like a pot of honey.

Laura McCaughan (8)
St Patrick & St Brigid's Primary School, Ballycastle

Van Gogh's Favourite Colour

Yellow looks like angels' wings.
Feels like Cocker Spaniels' fur.
Sounds like summer beginning.
Smells like yellow roses in a vase.
Tastes like bitter lemon and ice.

A field full of buttercups and sunshine.
A magnificent lion, his name is Yellow Flower.
Bright and golden like the sun.
His mane was like buttercups and primroses.
Such a beautiful scene.
It could be a dream.

Caitilin Gormley (8)
St Patrick & St Brigid's Primary School, Ballycastle

Mouse Hunter

Night breaks, morning wakes.
It's then his homeward journey makes.

Wings as white as snow.
Mice look nice to him, you know.

The barn owl sits under moonlight.
The barn owl has brilliant eyesight.

His flight is quick and silent.
He is very violent.

Woe betide mice who get in his way.
They'll never see the light of day.

Danielle McMichael (8)
St Patrick & St Brigid's Primary School, Ballycastle

Darkness

I am in my room, trying to get some sleep
Then I hear something, it sounds like a creak
It must be the stairs going to sleep
This is the house at night!

The silver moon lights up my room
I feel a shiver going down my back
Then I hear something . . .
A great big smash
But it must be the wind, the draught from the window
Making the shutters swing and clash.
Yes, this is the house at night.

The night is so quiet
I hear myself breathing,
I feel so tired and weary
But the house is so still and eerie
I pull the quilt around my head
And snuggle deep into my bed
Because this is the house at night!

Rachel McGuigan (10)
St Patrick & St Brigid's Primary School, Ballycastle

Barn Owl Acrostic

B arn owl flies at night.
A nimals beware!
R un away or you'll be caught.
N o mouse is safe.

O wls hunt quietly.
W ings are silent.
L ight of the moon helps him.

Alanna O'Donnell (8)
St Patrick & St Brigid's Primary School, Ballycastle

Darkness

Trying to get some sleep
Late in the night
But I hear a creak
It must be a door out of sight
This is the house at night.

Drip, drip is that the tap water
Or is it a zombie slaughterer
Coming to get me?
Grr, woof, woof is that the dog
Or is it a werewolf up in the fog?
This is the house at night.

Sizzle, sizzle, sizzle is that the heat turning off
Or is it a cobra coming to strangle me?
There's a shadow at my window
Somebody's coming to get me
I snuggle under my quilt but it's just a tree
So this is the house at night.

Sianine McGowan (11)
St Patrick & St Brigid's Primary School, Ballycastle

Swift Wing

All mice are out of sight
When the barn owl hunts at night.

The barn owl sleeps in daylight.
The barn owl hunts at night.

In the night the barn owl hunts for prey.
His wings are very quiet, I'd say.

Hugh Neill (8)
St Patrick & St Brigid's Primary School, Ballycastle

The House At Night

I hear noises under my bed
I think it's going to bite my head
Creak, creak goes the door
Someone's standing on the floor.
This is the house at night.

Something's outside, it's big and tall
There's a shadow on my bedroom wall.
Something's crawling up my ear
I've got a horrendous fear.
Someone gripped my arm real tight
This is the house at night.

Lying in my bed
Weird noises going round my head.
Knock, knock on the door
Is it a lion? I hear it roar.
It's starting to get light
This is the house at night.

Shannen McGarry (11)
St Patrick & St Brigid's Primary School, Ballycastle

Manchester United

Man United are the greatest team ever to play,
With Best, they usually beat the rest.
Charlton could hit some shots and hit the target,
Beckham used to pass like no one else
And Giggs and Ronaldo can worry any defence.
Rio is like a brick wall in our back line,
And Howard is one of the best keepers in the world.
That's why we are the best.

Diarmaid Hill (10)
St Patrick & St Brigid's Primary School, Ballycastle

Things That Give Me A Fright

It's most scary when it's dark at night
And everything is out of sight
The wind moans and groans
Like an old man's bones
The door creaks
And the tap leaks
These are the things that give me a fright
This is the house at night.

It's most scary when it's dark at night
And everything is out of sight
The leaves are rustling and the branches sway
Oh no, is there a ghost coming this way?
The central heating is banging and lets out a yelp
Or is it my mum and dad shouting for help?
These are the things that give me a fright
This is the house at night.

It's most scary when it's dark at night
And everything is out of sight
My alarm clock ticks
Or is it a burglar walking over sticks?
There are sharks swimming round my bed
Or is it all just in my head?
These are the things that give me a fright
Yes, this is the house at night.

Maeve McIlroy (11)
St Patrick & St Brigid's Primary School, Ballycastle

Summer

S is for the summer breeze.
U is for the umbrella to keep the sun out
M is for music to listen to
M is for milk to get you fit for running
E is for the elephant that comes from the zoo
R is for radio to listen to all during the summer.

Jacqueline McAuley (10)
St Patrick & St Brigid's Primary School, Ballycastle

There Is A Monster Under My Bed

There is a monster under my bed
I threw an axe under my bed
Hoping it is dead
It makes no more sound
Is it dead? Is it dead?

The noise starts again
I sit in one place thinking how to kill him
I went and got a butcher knife
I threw it under the bed
The noise stopped again
Is it dead? Is it dead?

The noise started again
I really got mad
I went and got a bomb
I put it under my bed
I ran out of the house
Right into the country and detonated it
It was dead! It was dead!
And so was the rest of my family!

Niall Caldwell (10)
St Patrick & St Brigid's Primary School, Ballycastle

Ballycastle Bay

My daddy has a speedboat,
He zooms along the bay.
Sometimes he leaves us on the beach
Where we can jump and play.
We build sandcastles very high
They seem to reach up to the sky.
We get sad when the sun goes down because
We flatten our sandcastles to the ground.
Oh, how sad we can be.
When we have to leave the sea.

Gemma Molloy (10)
St Patrick & St Brigid's Primary School, Ballycastle

Jurassic Jungle

C ompsognathus, a dino very small,
O viraptor who eats the eggs of all.
M egalosaurus, the first discovered beast,
P lateosaurus eats his leafy feast.
S tegosaurus, his plates made him tall, but his brain was small.
O rnithomimus who was so fast,
G igantosaurus was one of the last.
N otoceratops, he took some lives,
A llosaurus, with teeth like knives.
T yrannosaurus, he was king!
H adrosaurus' tail had a sting.
U tharaptor had a very big brain,
S eismosaurus, with neck high as a crane.

Daniel McKinley (10)
St Patrick & St Brigid's Primary School, Ballycastle

Motocross

Motocross is my favourite sport,
It's far better than running around a tennis court.
Losing is the worst part,
The person who beat me thinks they're smart.

A back marker swerved in front of me
And my goggles had ran out of roll-offs so I couldn't see,
So I threw them off and it started to rain,
Then it got windier to make it even more of a pain.

The best part is winning, which I do a lot
And the best bike on the track, I have got,
I've got a tonne of trophies; most are for first place,
In the hall where I keep them
We're running out of space!

Luke Stuart (10)
St Patrick & St Brigid's Primary School, Ballycastle

The Victorian Farm Boy

There was a boy who worked on a farm
He had no bed so he slept in a barn
To keep him warm he wrapped his feet in straw
For food he had a turnip raw.
He doesn't earn a lot of money
For his age he is really quite scrawny.

His name is Jim, nobody likes him
His master has no heart
All he calls him is a, 'Useless wee clart.'
Jim likes to talk to the cows
The farmer and his wife are always having rows.

His favourite animal is the donkey
His master says he acts the monkey
His ears are big, his nose is small
He looks quite weird, all in all.

Eamonn McCaughan (10)
St Patrick & St Brigid's Primary School, Ballycastle

Sports

Sports are fun
In some you run.
Others you swim
And sometimes you win.
Congratulations if you do . . .
You may get a bike - brand new
Or perhaps a bowl of cold . . .
Stew!
But whichever you are . . .
Cheetah or snail,
Or possibly in a sinking speedboat . . .
Bail, bail, bail!

David Herald (10)
St Patrick & St Brigid's Primary School, Ballycastle

Sweets

S is for Smarties, I love Smarties
W is for we all love sweets
E is for eating we all eat, eat sweets
E is for Extra, a nice minty chewing gum
T is for treats, sweets are really good treats
S is for sour, everyone likes sour sweets.

Kirsty Mooney (10)
St Patrick & St Brigid's Primary School, Ballycastle

Places

Sad little Jane,
Went to Spain,
It didn't rain,
Now she's happy again.

My friend Brittany,
Went to Italy,
She sent a postcard to me,
Now I'm as happy as can be.

A boy called Brian,
Came to Ireland,
He got bitten by a lion,
Now he's cryin'.

Little Jimmy Blair,
Lives in Ballyclare,
He bought a mare,
With dark brown hair.

These people play with me,
This year we're off to Jersey,
To have fun by the sea,
And have fish and chips for tea.

Heather Gault (10)
Tildarg Primary School

My Pets

My pets are funny,
They have tails on their head;

My pets are fun,
They can't catch a ball;

My pets are stupid,
They have no feet;

My pets are five,
They have five eyes;

My pets are brown,
They have no fur;

My pets are in my head,
Don't believe anything I've said!

Nicole McConnell (9)
Tildarg Primary School

Winter

Winter is a nice time of year,
People have cold ears,
People wear lots of clothes,
People have red noses.

People eat lots of sweets,
They eat and eat and eat,
Children have lots of fun,
People eat a lot of buns.

People make a lot of snowmen,
It will be very cold then,
Don't be bad and don't be bold,
Wrap up warm I have been told.

Carlyn Tosh (10)
Tildarg Primary School

Scary Monsters

When you look out of your window at night,
Beware because it might give you a fright,
The ghosts and ghouls and even the vampires,
Go round bursting your tyres.

But the worst things of all,
If you are quite tall,
Is if you hear a big boom,
They've taken you to a tomb.

They've made a big lake,
So you can't escape,
If you even dare to talk,
They make you smell a sock.

You're there till you die,
So give a big sigh,
Don't try to get away,
Because you're there for the rest of your days.

Shauna-Lee Warwick (9)
Tildarg Primary School

My Parents

She's pretty funny
Cunning and smart
She speaks from the heart
My mummy.

He's happy and never is a baddie
Loving and sweet
He'd give me his seat
My daddy.

So together
Here they are
The greatest parents in the whole world
Ha! Ha! They're all mine!

Sammi Jo Millar (11)
Tildarg Primary School

My Husband, A Pirate

In the day, my husband sails a boat,
Wearing his old, woolly, brown coat.
He only has one eye,
Though, he's a very good spy.
He has a big sword,
But he sometimes gets bored.
He travels the seas,
To bring treasure back for me!

At night my husband comes home,
In the dark, all alone.
He desperately wanted some tea,
So he let himself in with a skeleton key.
He says he doesn't like ships,
But that didn't come from my lips!
He always causes a riot,
My husband, a pirate.

David Kelly (10)
Tildarg Primary School

Wintertime

Winter is a time of snow
And all the cold winds blow,
You need to be bold,
Because it's freezing cold!

Coats, gloves, scarves and hats,
You had better wear,
But when I am in, I sit on the mat
And pat my warm, furry cat.

Christmas is near,
It's almost here,
I put up a tree,
With lovely decorations for all to see.

Tori Wallace (10)
Tildarg Primary School

My Family

I have a big sister,
She is called Keri,
She gets blisters,
People call her hairy Keri.

I have a big brother,
He brings me PVA glue,
I wish I had another,
Aaron's favourite colour is blue.

Now what about my mummy?
She often goes shopping,
She gets a sore tummy,
She likes to do the mopping.

Oh, I forgot about my dad!
He usually goes to work,
He often drives me mad,
He always gives me a smirk.

Now, I have two cats,
One called Fidget and one called Dike,
They both are very fat,
Their claws are like spikes.

Katie Cummings (9)
Tildarg Primary School

Seasons On The Farm

In spring little lambs are born
And farmers are planting seeds for corn.

In summer farmers are watering the crops,
So they will soon pop.

In autumn the farmers are tutting,
Because they have to do the cutting.

In winter the farmers are rounding up the sheep,
So they can come in and have a cosy sleep.

Emma Patterson (8)
Tildarg Primary School

My Family And Pet

When my dad gets out of bed,
He tells a joke that is funny,
He always takes my favourite 'ted',
It is my cuddly bunny.

When my mum comes up the path,
She likes the rail to hold,
She needs a warm bath,
Because she is always cold.

When Peter gets up it is midday,
He has a bath,
He goes to Granny's and he goes away,
Down the path.

When Debbie takes the bathroom,
You won't get in it,
You have to wait in another room,
So go away and sit!

When Kelly goes shopping,
She scares me a bit,
She is always hopping,
But don't tell her I said it!

When Karl comes to nip,
He's like a bee,
Tell him to take a tip:
Nobody can do it like me.

My dog is called Spot,
He loves to play,
I like it a lot,
He'll never go astray!

Stephanie McDowell (10)
Tildarg Primary School

My Cat, Sweep

My cat, Sweep,
He's always asleep,
He's always on the mat,
He's just that kind of cat.

My cat, Sweep,
He likes to eat meat,
When he comes home at night,
He gives me quite a fright.

My cat, Sweep,
He likes to leap,
When he comes home, he feels quite alone,
Until he sees our garden gnome.

My cat, Sweep,
He sometimes creeps into the bushes to eat,
When it's night and he's outside,
He goes up to the slide to hide.

Vicki Manson (9)
Tildarg Primary School

My Little Brother

My little brother
Annoys my mother,
She began to cry,
But my little brother asked why
As he was eating a pie.

Then she grabbed him and threw him in the sky,
He landed in the pig sty,
She said, 'Get to bed
Or you will have a sore head!'

Stuart Patton (9)
Tildarg Primary School

Monster In My Bedroom

I was lying in my bed,
When I saw a scary head.
It had five eyes and a nose,
I couldn't keep my eyes closed.

I got up to see,
What could I see?
It was in below my bed,
I was hugging Ted!

As I crept over,
It seemed to come closer.
I stepped over again,
Then it heard the rain.

It scared him and he was gone,
What happened to the monster?

Susan Bates (10)
Tildarg Primary School

Autumnal Tankas

Leaves swaying like swings,
Leaves fluttering like fairies,
They play like children.
Dance a lot and fly like birds.
Then they go to bed and wait.

Animals sleeping.
All cuddly and warm they sleep.
Conkers fall off trees.
Coming out of spiky shells.
And wait for autumn again.

Jessica Foley (9)
Tir na Nog Primary School

Winter

Winter is a cold, old man,
He blows and freezes all around me,
He is weak and shrivelled,
He is lonely as he creeps in the snow,
Looking for somewhere to rest his head.
His breath is like fog,
That twinkles through the night,
He is like a star,
Floating in the air,
To warn people that winter is here.

Peter Dixon (8)
Tir na Nog Primary School

The Famine

Fatigue, tiredness, weakness caused by deadly diseases
And starvation.
A blight over the potatoes caused them to fail.
Malnutrition, no nutrients, very unhealthy, they were feeling miserable.
In the workhouses, people were suffering and dying.
Not many people survived the famine, it was a traumatic time.
Evicted, desperate, unhappy, terrible - and
Feelings of hopelessness.

Colette Kelly (9)
Tir na Nog Primary School

Snowflakes In The Air

Snowflakes in the air,
They twist and twirl as they fall down.
They are see-through like glass,
They look like wheels as they tumble to the ground.

Samuel McGookin (8)
Tir na Nog Primary School

Snowflakes

Snowflakes in the air,
Slowly falling like twinkling stars and breaking glass.
They sound like the sharp singing of birds,
They flutter while they twinkle,
They float down like angels,
They twist and twirl
And die when they land.

Shannon McCrea (7)
Tir na Nog Primary School

Winter Trees Rondelet

The tree has sap.
When leaves fall you can't hear the sound.
The tree has sap.
In winter the tree has a nap,
Leaves go around when coming down,
Leaves flow when coming to the ground,
The tree has sap.

Karen Dempsey (8)
Tir na Nog Primary School

Winter Trees Rondelet

Trees stand dormant,
They sway and twist like they don't care.
Trees stand dormant.
In under the coarse bark ants crawl,
From prong to twig to twiglet bare.
Leaves fall because cold is in the air.
Trees stand dormant.

Fionnuala Carmichael (10)
Tir na Nog Primary School

The Wind

The wind is like a thunderous gush,
Making trees flow side to side.
Wind is a mysterious blast of air.
We don't know how old the wind is.
We can't tell if it is a he or a she.
The wind is disguised we cannot tell anything.
When the wind is disguised we cannot tell anything.
When the wind enters with its ghostly games,
Swinging to and fro with his destructive force.
He destroys our plants,
He damages people and their homes.
He doesn't even realise that he is.
The wind keeps on doing it, it never stops!

Shannon Neale (8)
Tir na Nog Primary School

The Wind

The wind is a forceful, energetic weather,
That's like an angry, raging, destructive bull
That just wants to kill, kill, kill.
Or it could be a playful little kitten or a calm, peaceful butterfly.
It could be invisible, mysterious, ghostly,
A phantom that haunts you at night when you are in bed.
It could be a tremendous king that rules the world.
The grass is like people that get out of the wind's way.
The trees are like the servants that bow down
When the wind comes their way.
The daffodils are like the wives.

Erin Fowler (8)
Tir na Nog Primary School

Wind

A ghostly, lively, powerful force,
Rushing through the trees,
Scattering everything in its course
And pushing waves on the seas.
It can be a bull that can kill,
It can be a kitten that's gentle and still.
It comes in an outburst,
It comes in a blast,
It bends down the trees when it goes past.
A prankster, a joker, a boisterous thing,
Sometimes I hear it whistle and sing.
Sometimes I hear it in bed tucked up tight,
I look out the window and there is nothing in sight.
I look out again and I hear it whistle,
Then I saw it had blown down a thistle.
It blows the washing up and down
And the daffodils with their golden crown.
All my friends have had enough,
But I don't think he's really that tough!

Catherine Kelly (11)
Tir na Nog Primary School

The Wind

It's like a brother taking your books.
Sometimes it can be like a quiet flower standing still.
Most of the time it can be very destructive,
Like a ram stamping his feet on the ground.
It sometimes can behave badly, getting the cars
And bikes off the road.
Sometimes it can move trees and twigs.
Also it can trip people over onto the ground.
If you have an ice cream, it can blow it off the cone.
Sometimes it can blow very hard, its cheeks can go red.

Katy Moutray (9)
Tir na Nog Primary School

The Wind

The wind is mysterious
It has power to move things.
Bending plants like they're bowing to a leader.
Shaking windows like they had 50 hands.
It's always very energetic.
Useful to birds to make them fly.
Charges like a bull on wintery nights.
It blows paper in people's faces as a joke.
Wind can destroy life.
It has a ghostly voice.

Thomas McGookin (11)
Tir na Nog Primary School